Disformations

thinking|media

Series Editors:

Bernd Herzogenrath
Patricia Pisters

DISFORMATIONS

Affects, Media, Literature

Tomáš Jirsa

BLOOMSBURY ACADEMIC
NEW YORK • LONDON • OXFORD • NEW DELHI • SYDNEY

BLOOMSBURY ACADEMIC
Bloomsbury Publishing Inc
1385 Broadway, New York, NY 10018, USA
50 Bedford Square, London, WC1B 3DP, UK
29 Earlsfort Terrace, Dublin 2, Ireland

BLOOMSBURY, BLOOMSBURY ACADEMIC and the Diana logo are
trademarks of Bloomsbury Publishing Plc

First published in the United States of America 2021
This paperback edition published in 2022

Cover design by www.ironicitalics.com
Cover image courtesy of the Fondo Emilio Uranga, Departamento de Filosofía,
Universidad de Guanajuato

Library of Congress Cataloging-in-Publication Data
Names: Jirsa, Tomáš, 1983- author.
Title: Disformations: affects, media, literature / Tomáš Jirsa.
Description: New York : Bloomsbury Academic, 2021. | Series: Thinking media
| Includes bibliographical references and index.
Identifiers: LCCN 2020033918 | ISBN 978-1-5013-6234-7 (hardback) | ISBN
978-1-5013-6233-0 (epub) | ISBN 978-1-5013-6232-3 (pdf)
Subjects: LCSH: Form (Philosophy) in art. | Form (Philosophy) in
literature. | Form (Philosophy) | Affect (Psychology) in art. | Affect
(Psychology) in literature. | Affect (Psychology)
Classification: LCC NX650.F67 J57 2021 | DDC 701/.8–dc23
LC record available at https://lccn.loc.gov/2020033918

ISBN: HB: 978-1-5013-6234-7
     PB: 978-1-5013-7489-0
     ePDF: 978-1-5013-6232-3
     eBook: 978-1-5013-6233-0

Series: Thinking Media

Typeset by Deanta Global Publishing Services, Chennai, India

To find out more about our authors and books visit www.bloomsbury.com
and sign up for our newsletters.

To Veronika and Zoe

CONTENTS

FIGURES

ACKNOWLEDGMENTS

Since this book is an endeavor to pursue intriguing, often disconcerting, yet always creative encounters that produce new forms in motion, people whom I want to thank here have had precisely such an impact on my work. They came or appeared right at those moments when I thought I already knew, turned my would-be knowledge and impetuous ideas upside down, let me fumble while endowing me with countless impulses that I usually did not get at first, but that eventually turned into a fruitful path to be followed. Briefly, all of them have been a cherished and radically productive disturbance to my own intellectual confinement, and encounters with them have shaped both this book and myself.

First of all, I wish to wholeheartedly thank Bernd Herzogenrath and Patricia Pisters for giving me the opportunity to publish this book within the Bloomsbury series Thinking Media. Without Bernd's enthusiasm and scholarly generosity, these pages would remain just an eternal work in progress. My gratitude goes also to the Bloomsbury editors, Katie Gallof and Erin Duffy, who were exceptionally helpful and kind during the whole publishing process.

Among colleagues, mentors, and friends, who read different parts of this book at its early stage and provided a useful suggestion, an insightful comment, a striking recommendation, or a vital encouragement, my sincere thanks go to Josef Vojvodík, Josef Fulka, Marcel Arbeit, Josef Šebek, Jiří Anger, Christiane Voss, Ross Etherton, Jerrold E. Hogle, Peter Zusi, Jussi Parikka, Alexandra Irimia, and, in memoriam, Patrizia Lombardo.

My thinking about the entanglements between forms, affects, and media is particularly indebted to the generosity of Internationales Kolleg für Kulturtechnikforschung und Medienphilosophie (IKKM) in Weimar, whose proud fellow I was for a couple of months in 2015 and 2017. Besides being a tremendously inspiring platform for the contemporary media philosophy and study of cultural techniques, it is also an outstanding center of *la gaia scienza* that exceeds rigid academic protocols and boundaries on the way to opening a thought-provoking interdisciplinary dialogue. For giving me an invaluable opportunity to make part of this dialogue, I am immensely grateful to both IKKM directors, Lorenz Engell and Bernhard Siegert. One of the precious gems of the fellowships was meeting Antonio Somaini, not just a brilliant scholar and delightful companion but also a generous mentor. The day-and-night Weimar conversations with Antonio gifted me with many astute suggestions that I gleefully used here.

Another compelling fellowship during which I was given a necessary time, space, and inspiration to make decisive changes to both conception and structure of this book was provided by Amsterdam School for Cultural Analysis (ASCA), which invited me as Visiting Scholar in Spring 2019. For this beautiful period in Amsterdam, my profound thanks go to Abe Geil, Patricia Pisters, and Eloe Kingma. For continual institutional support and confidence in my work, I owe gratitude to the Faculty of Arts of Palacký University Olomouc, my scholarly home since 2016, and in particular to its former dean Jiří Lach.

At one especially difficult moment in my scholarly life, Ernst van Alphen, for whom I was then just an anonymous stranger and one of his myriad readers, was supportive enough to give me his trust, sharing his contacts as well as editorial background, and made possible a collaboration for which I will be forever thankful. Not only did I have a chance to coedit with Ernst the collection *How to Do Things with Affects*, whose main concept of the affective triggers underlies this book's major argument, but his critical yet encouraging reading of my work also led me to substantially reshape many unclear points in the manuscript.

Among those who read carefully both this book's proposal and the initial drafts of some of its chapters is Pietro Conte, whose charming erudition, bright analytical observations, and essentially transdisciplinary suggestions were of an invaluable help to the whole book. Even though I met Abe Geil at a later stage of editing this manuscript, his wonderful help with and close reading of an important part of this book were all the more intense. Abe's affirmative intellectual support and magnanimous spirit have contributed a great deal not only to these pages but also to other related scholarly projects.

A close reader par excellence, whose many sharp insights and intriguing questions literally exploded the original conception of this book to ultimately reform it into a new theoretical inquiry, is Eugenie Brinkema. The wit of her rigorous scholarship, the polemic drive of her arguments, the enjoyable rhythm of her elegant writing but mainly her insistence on putting my argument front and center including generous suggestions how to go about it—all has inscribed its indelible traces into every single page of this book. Furthermore, encounters with Eugenie between Olomouc, Prague, and Amsterdam are a solid proof that meeting your favorite authors in person can be as cheering and fruitful as reading them.

An early version of Chapter 1 was published as "Affective Disfigurations: Faceless Encounters between Literary Modernism and the Great War" in *How to Do Things with Affects: Affective Triggers in Aesthetic Forms and Cultural Practices* (2019), edited by Ernst van Alphen and Tomáš Jirsa. Chapter 2 reuses material previously published in "Lost in Pattern: Rococo Ornament and Its Journey to Contemporary Art through Wallpaper" in *Where Is History Today? New Ways of Representing the Past* (2015), edited by Marcel Arbeit and Ian Christie, with considerable revision. Finally, Chapter 4 is an extended and substantially revised version of "Portrait of Absence: The Aisthetic Mediality of the Empty Chairs" in *Zeitschrift für Medien- und Kulturforschung* (2016). I thank the copyright holders of these previous publications for permitting me to revise them for this book.

A special note of thanks to the artists Michal Pěchouček and Jan Šerých for allowing me to reproduce their works.

WHEN FORMS FALL APART

AN INTRODUCTION

> Form would therefore always be derived from the look of the trace,
> which explains why it is so easy to pierce it, *undo* it, *explode* it.
>
> Catherine Malabou, *Plasticity at the Dusk of Writing*, 2010

We like to believe that forms have a shape that holds them together, gives them a name, and outlines the traces they leave in our mind. They do—usually. A boat is a floating board surrounded by water that can give us an oceanic feeling; a chair is a four-legged object always ready to seat a person; a piece of garbage is a refused thing that once served its purpose, was consumed, and now placidly dwells on a trash heap. But what does the same boat tell us when left at the mercy of the untamed elements, when smashed to pieces by the giant snout of Moby Dick, when washed up, all rotten, on shore? Is the formal arrangement of the chair identical when finally not taken by someone who was desperately awaited? Does such a void make the chair empty or simply a chair *an sich*, and what if, as Wittgenstein envisions, "I go to fetch it, and it suddenly disappears from sight?" (2009: 42). And finally, what if the still piece of garbage is taken from the ground, examined as a mediaphilosophical problem, or used as a framework through which the human history can be read? Different situations make different relations that rewrite, reform, and open forms to novel formations showing something we did not know yet.

Such an opening of forms toward the not-yet-known exceeds by far the realm of tangible objects and can take place as part of any aesthetic experience. Consider, for example, a moment of listening to music: the tune is appealing, its sequence of chords seems in a perfect order, the pitch, cadence, and instrumentation sound just right—and then, all of a sudden, something goes wrong: the tone gets out of tune, the rhythm goes scattered, and a new annoying instrumental motif gradually becomes dominant. What established itself as harmony has been invaded by disharmony, not so much its opposite, an incorrectness, or even destruction but rather its reverse, disturbing counterpart, and radical difference, coming both from within and without while subverting the previous logical ordering. For disharmony that "replaces the place of harmony and attunement," as Heidegger notes in his lectures on Schelling's conception of evil, is nothing else but "the wrong tone which enters the whole" (Withy 2015: 144). It is precisely this wrong tone—disrupting the formal integrity and harmony as it does and yet opening, reforming, and reconfiguring the formal wholeness—along with the theoretical potential of its performative force and affective agency that this book investigates. And that these formal dissonances, distortions, and disturbances are driven by specific affective operations that push the recognizable forms to the limits of representation, is the following chapters' main claim.

Arguing for a novel concept of "disformations" that involves affective operations based on the generative deformation of forms, the task of this book is to address the question of how modern and contemporary aesthetic forms can capture, mediate, and unfold the affective agency that disrupts the recognizable forms on the way to producing new formations, and what theoretical consequences these formal disturbances offer to the aesthetic and mediaphilosophical thinking. In order to explore the particular sites of *disformations* across intermedia figures in literature, the visual, and the audiovisual arts, the following chapters take us through four different encounters with the twisted formations whose shape, motion, and affective force pose a problem *for*, *of*, and *to* form, encounters which arise from the intrusion of disharmony into the harmony of forms. To do so, the aesthetic media that allow these encounters will be approached not only as artistic objects to be analyzed and reflected upon but also as thinking media in their own right. Invested in the endeavor of the series *Thinking Media* under the auspices of which this book appears—to explore the philosophical qualities and impacts of each medium while emphasizing the material basis of such mediations—the following inquiries build upon the mediaphilosophical notion that arts and media constitute a form of thinking, *do the work of thinking*, while arguing that this thinking is essentially *performative*.

Yet, what does it mean to claim that forms think? To pursue such thinking, should we comply with the omnipresent and, in fact, omnivorous "similitude to meaning," which Adorno claims in relation to Samuel Beckett's writing?[1] Or, even more fatally, do we have to fall back into the allegorical reading that, according to Hans Ulrich Gumbrecht, approaches the cultural texts as stockpiles of the ready-made "philosophical arguments or agendas" and seeks "to free ideational content from the bothersome complexities of form" (2012: 13)? Not necessarily, for once we shift from the representational regime of forms and affects to their performativity—to what forms and affects really *do* and how they *work*—this force of art has no more so much to do with a scholastic decoding of some intentional and strictly metaphysical message. To disentangle from the certitudes of those preexistent agendas, the already known themes and significations, that is, in favor of uncovering the aesthetic media's work of thinking, one just needs to undertake what Žižek calls the "dialectical analysis" whose fundamental gesture is "a step back from content to form, that suspension of content which renders form visible anew" (2008a: 153). To think the generative "wrong tone" sustaining the unsettling disharmony of forms is to reflect upon their media conditions and consequences. By shifting the accent from the forms and media objects in their alleged autonomy to the encounters with them, this book approaches *disformations* in the non-essentialist terms and in their *mediality*—that is in their "underlying materialities, dispositives and performances that accompany medial processes" (Mersch 2013: 208). Subscribing to the key impetus of cultural analysis that in order to be useful concepts need to engage in an interdisciplinary dialogue and "travel" between various scholarly discourses (Bal 2002), the major concept of *disformations*—describing processes that open form toward disturbances through affective operations—is discussed within the rich theoretical framework including cultural affect theory, media philosophy, literary studies, and psychoanalysis.

And here lies the reason for this somewhat odd neologism of *disformations* that ties the negative, privative prefix "dis" with the noun of action capturing an act of giving or taking form, a shape in its unfolding into a new structure and arrangement and whose task is to link disturbances to form to the affective operations. For what this concept attempts to underscore is that the affective operations, engendered within the unsettling work of forms and activated upon encounters with the unknown formations, do not destroy the form but rather *dis*turb and *dis*tort it, reverse and reform—and hence reformulate the form. Expanding on the etymological root of the Latin *dis* that, as the *Oxford English Dictionary* tells us, contains the meanings of "apart," "asunder," "in twain," (*OED*, s.v. "dis") the semantic charge of the concept of *disformations* is twofold: to involve a generatively *dis*ruptive intrusion of the confusing "wrong tone" into form and hence a certain *dis*harmony which corrupts—and, indeed, brings a kind of performative "dissing," a formal *dis*respect to—an already established formal whole on the way to producing new but no less *dis*turbing *formations*. And to show that these formal sites which abound with activity, capacity, and latency are grounded in the affective work of forms that permanently hinders and short-circuits representation—for how to positively re-present something that is just taking shape, which is at odds with its proper name, what language is struggling to come to terms with?—in favor of performative mechanisms which are driven by their mediality. If affects stand not only for "those encounters between bodies that involve a change" but also for "generative irruption[s], potentially kindling transitions from established understandings towards new thoughts and new discursive and practical moves," and therefore provide "a dynamic reservoir of possibility, spheres of potential—what is *formative but not yet formed*" (Slaby and Mühlhoff 2019: 27, 38; emphasis added), then the coinage of *disformations* which interconnects the formal work of affects with the affective work of forms seems justifiable.

So, how to understand *disformations* as affective operations that open form to not-yet-known formations and mediations and in what ways does the concept allow to think forms and affects together? To answer these questions and outline the conceptual trajectories through which the following chapters link the disturbances to form with the operative agency of affects, this book is based upon three major premises. The first premise is that in order for the formal disturbances to say something new about form, they need to be situated neither outside nor before but *within* the form's performative motion. Approaching these deformations not as a destruction of form but as generative reformations opens up an avenue for addressing the aesthetic forms that reach the limits of representation. The second premise holds that the formal disturbances *trigger* the affective operations that, in turn, reshape, restructure, and rewrite the forms into new formations. These affective operations thus contain a double movement of the formal work of affects but also the affective work of forms. Since *disformations* are not just aesthetically but also theoretically generative, the third premise of this book involves what Jacques Aumont describes as the "thinking through figures" done by cinematic images (1996: 170),[2] except that what this book argues for is that this work of thinking *through* and *with* figures is done by all aesthetic media, whether they belong to modern literature, contemporary audiovisual arts, or classic cinema. In other words, the aesthetic forms do the work of thinking through the intermedia figures.

Disformations Open Form to New Formations

What happens when a form falls apart? Does it become formless? And how to understand the force that drives such a deformation that, ultimately, opens the form to the unprecedented formations? First of all, we will get nowhere if we stick with the received idea of form as a stable and inherent ontological category, one that is inseparably linked to the identity of an object or a subject, be it a human body, a nonhuman animal, a petal, a rock, or a flame. In order for form thus conceived to be recognizable, it needs to meet two essential conditions: first, being endowed with a generic structure and shape; second, corresponding to some kind of empirical experience that, ideally, gives the form a name. In light of this Neoplatonic view, the form occurs as "a body without which there is neither spirit nor life, a signifier without which there is no signified" (Plana 2010: 29). Yet this perspective is but one among many other ways to think the notion of form, one whose countless concepts have pervaded both humanities and sciences throughout the twentieth century until now and, in a surprising albeit usually unintentional congruity, resonated with and complement each other. According to the biologist and philosopher René Thom, the form is to be understood "only on the basis of perturbations and shocks it produces within the diffusion of a certain flux across the space" (1992: 25).[3] Even though this implies that to analyze such a form in flux one needs to halt its unspecified stream of events and particles for a certain amount of time, an important criterion that is less ontological and rather operational arises here: to consider any form at all requires focusing on its activity *in relation to* its surrounding.

Building upon the idea of the formal and—as the telling title of his groundbreaking work *Vie des formes* (*The Life of Forms in Art*, 1934) suggests—*organic* activity, the art historian Henri Focillon introduced the form as a living, ever-morphing, and self-generating element that evolves over time and survives across history and various cultural contexts. And because in his view not solely aesthetic but any existing form is actually unthinkable without its essential movement, Focillon dubbed the form intriguingly as the "curve of an activity" (*la courbe d'une activité*), containing a creative principle of an artwork but also the one of space and time, matter and spirit. As a result, "[n]ot only may every activity be comprehended and defined to the extent that it assumes form and inscribes its curve in space and time, but life itself, furthermore, is essentially a creator of forms" (1992: 33).[4] Studying the formal metamorphoses and their survivals in various moments of cultural history, Focillon's thesis on the life of forms shows much more than a radical shift from the positivist, dominantly historicizing, approach of nineteenth-century art history. His notion of mobile forms—*forms in motion*—provides us with a speculative impulse to think the aesthetic forms not as ontologically given representational units but rather from *within* their dynamic transformations and proliferating movement.

It would not be difficult to trace this line of reasoning which understands form not as stable entity but as an organic process both retrospectively—through Bergson's notion of the *élan vital* from his *Creative Evolution* (1907) as a foundational evolutionary principle of the living organisms to the dynamic conception of morphology concerned with the nature's perpetual transformations, as pioneered by Goethe at the end of the eighteenth century;[5] to Aristotle's *hylomorphism* as explained in his *Physics* (*c.* 335–323 BCE)—and forward—from the little-known "metabiology of art" by Wladimir Weidlé (1957) based on the structural analogies between the cellular tissue of living organisms and the mobile "units of tension" of art forms; to Adolf Portmann's work on the self-expression of living beings (1964) and his impact on biosemiotics; to Tim Ingold's comparison between the organic forms' morphogenetic field and the "field of forces" wherein "the form of the artefact evolves" (2000: 345); or to the psychoanalytical works of Pierre Fédida who argues that nothing but life and vitality of form is what allows any perceivable action (2000: 115). For all its theoretical power, however, the vitalist view risks covering too much of the formal dynamic into the metaphors of organicism and natural growth. To follow a radically disturbing and not always organic process that disrupts form from both without and within—the intricate violence of form, that is—and the moments when the forms fall apart while revealing their unexpected reverse, it seems necessary to delve into different discourses as well.

Among the many attempts to shed light on the disruptive force of forms, two powerful conceptual inquiries appear around the turn of the twenty-first century: the first one stakes itself on paying tribute to and reformulating the Bataillean modernist notion of the *formless* and the second endeavor builds upon Hegel's idea of *plasticity*. While the former was undertaken simultaneously, on the one hand by Georges Didi-Huberman (1995), and on the other by Yve-Alain Bois and Rosalind Krauss (1997), the latter has been tackled by Catherine Malabou.[6] Let us begin with the former case as the notion of the "formless" pre-echoes many features which the latter concept succinctly contains. I will also argue that the debate which took place around the mid-1990s calls not so much for revisiting as for reorienting toward a field that the scholarly discourse of the formless left almost completely aside: the one of the affective agency.

What became a key concept of Georges Bataille's materialist philosophy was first introduced in 1929 in the revue *Documents* under the entry of its regular section "Critical Dictionary," and gained a simple name *Informe* (Formless). While his well-known theorem posits that the *"formless* is not only an adjective having a given *meaning*, but a term that serves to bring things down in the world, generally requiring that each thing have its form," Bataille concludes that "affirming that the universe resembles nothing and is only *formless* amounts to saying that the universe is something like a spider or spit" (Bataille 1985: 31). When parsing Bataille's writings from which this anti-aesthete—rather than a counter-aesthetic—stance arises, Denis Hollier notes that Bataille "was able to save the violence of desire from the temptation of form," thus linking the form with a continuity and fixity of discourse, which led him to aim at a "transgression of form" (1992: 24). But does a form really need to transgress itself in order not to be trapped in an abstract system, a pre-arranged order, or an idealization? In other words, do we have to play down the notion of form to show the potential of its reverse?

A speculatively rich answer is to be found in Didi-Huberman's book *La Ressemblance informe ou le gai savoir visuel selon Georges Bataille* (Formless Resemblance, or Georges Bataille's Gay Visual Science, 1995), whose title clearly shows that the crucial figure of Bataille's subversive thinking—the formless—produces a radical epistemological break for "what demonstrates itself to be a visual relationship, similarity or disproportion—the disproportionate resemblance, that is—acquires the capacity to shake up the knowing itself and to create an unprecedented knowledge" (1995: 39). According to Didi-Huberman, the formless operates as a latency of form, a disturbing possibility of its deformation and, at the same time, a proliferation of new forms in motion—a process that neither unfolds beyond the forms nor precedes them and that is not immanent to them but rather *takes place in touch* with the subject, because only the gaze and haptic contact have a paradoxical capacity to transform any shape into something unrecognizable, a capacity of the formless to suddenly "impose to any form the force of the dissimilar" (1995: 135). The formless as both a disruptive symptomatic quality of forms and a moment of the intrusion of the radically unknown into a recognizable form hence "lies at the very points of forms, where their contact is the most decisive, the most painful, the most disjointed

[le plus disloquant]" (1995: 268). What therefore differentiates the
formless from its usual negative understanding in terms of destruction,
a mushy abstraction, or simply an anti-form, is the very dialectic
between the aggressively deformative process on the one hand, and
the work of the formless within the form, on the other; an event that
generates a form throughout its deformation and could hence be
dubbed the "formlessnessing."[7]

By situating the process of the formless into the forms themselves,
Didi-Huberman commits a creative conceptual betrayal against Bataille's
original term, a betrayal that opens up a theoretical potential that I will
set on to elaborate in the first chapter. This conceptual move that could
be understood as a generative extension of Bataille's negativity is also
what differentiates Didi-Huberman from another reading of the term as
introduced by Bois and Krauss. In their catalogue to the 1996 exposition
at the Centre Georges Pompidou in Paris entitled *L'informe: mode
d'emploi* (*Formless: A User's Guide*), they posit the formless as an
operational, performative force of "declassification" at work in modern
and postmodern visual arts. In sound opposition to Didi-Huberman—
whose interpretation Bois somewhat hastily dismisses as a sort of vague
"metaphor" which is so large as to cover almost all modern figurative
art (1997: 79–81)—they see the formless as a negation of both the form
and the content, as "the operation that displaces both of these terms"
(1997: 15), and *use* it to "declassify the larger unities that are the very
stuff of art history: style, theme, chronology, and, finally, oeuvre as the
total body of an artist's work" (1997: 21). The reason why I subscribe
to Didi-Huberman's approach rather than to Krauss' and Bois' is that
whereas for the latter the performative force of the formless is essentially
iconoclastic, for the former it is *iconomorphic*, standing for a dialectical
process that engenders images through the labor of deformation. If
the aim of Krauss' and Bois' experiment was "putting the formless to
work in areas far from its place of origin, in displacing it in order to
sift modernist production by means of its sieve" (1997: 40), what has
arguably remained stuck in that sieve is the generative force of the
formless, a force that cannot be brought to the light until the formless is
seen as the opposite of the form.

In their attempt to revitalize this concept for the use of literary
studies, Patrick Crowley and Paul Hegarty situate the formless at the
level of both performativity and representation (as if to accommodate
Didi-Huberman's to Krauss and Bois' approach, one might suggest).
"*Informe* is at work within literary form, working at its limits both
from within (as formal anti-form) and from without (as interpretative

movement)" (2005: 111). The formless which basically stands for "an interruption of completion" (2005: 111) may hence be approached as an operational quality that thwarts the conventions of genre, and also provides us a with an analytical tool that is attuned to the forms that reach the limits of representation. What seems especially engaging and close to the inquiry of *Disformations* is Crowley's and Hegarty's emphasis on the generative deformations and their performative qualities whereby "the primacy of form can be disrupted through movement and the work of other forms that deform and displace" (2005: 109). But here, time and again, lies also a crucial problem of the Bataillean vocabulary; because if the *deformation as reformation* is what the formless calls forth, if the formless emerges as a *latency* of form that can manifest and unfold both within the form and outside, then such a process requires an appropriately differentiated concept that the term formless cannot anymore sustain—a concept that would not be burdened by the inescapable negativity of the suffix "less," that could step beyond not only the (misleading) semantic opposition between the form and its formless counterpart but also its modernist blueprint, a concept that would account for the deformation as a generative, dialectical encounter with form.

And it is this very dialectic not of form and its "other" but of this "other" *within* the form that lies at heart of Malabou's notion of *plasticity*. Taking her cue from the work of Hegel but also from a rich etymology of the adjective "plastic" that contains the "capacity to receive form and a capacity to produce form," she elaborates upon this double signification to compellingly probe it as a "speculative word" (2005: 9). The plasticity then "signifies the disruption and deflagration of presence, the 'explosive side of subjectivity,'" while functioning as "a *structure of transformation and destruction of presence and the present*" (2010: 9). In light of this dynamic, Malabou introduces—thus implicitly joining Thom's view on the non-static perturbative forms— the "metabolic power" of plasticity, that is "its capacity to *order transformation*" (2010: 21). Questioning her own assertions about plasticity from her earlier work *The Future of Hegel* (2005), where the word oscillates between two extreme manifestations of form, one crystallizing into a formal whole while the other referring to the power of annihilation and explosion of form, Malabou overcomes such a duality by proposing plasticity as "a wider hermeneutic instrument, a smuggler trafficking between dialectic, destruction, and deconstruction" (2010: 22). Could a mediaphilosophical problem ever be articulated in a sharper way?

The theoretical promise of this smuggler, permanently at the edge (of the law, of the rules), in between (territories and categories), and at the same time, both inside and outside (the field of its action), comes to the fore, especially when related to the disturbing motion of forms. More specifically, plasticity as "the form of alterity without transcendence" (2010: 66) replies to the permanent capacity of form, be it plastic or graphic, to be transformed and to impose its dynamic upon the ways it is thought. When looking back at our opening examples of the smashed boat, the empty chair, and the harmony deconstructed by a wrong tone, it becomes clear that the concept of plasticity, at the crux of which lies a permanent metamorphosis, embraces such degrees, stages, and situations of disturbances to form. Furthermore, by its emphasis on literature, which is nothing less than a plastic work of writing, this books joins Malabou's claim that the "plasticity is the metamorphosis of writing" in that it "*configures traces and erases them to form them, without however rigidifying them*" (2010: 61). Such a writing, always in the modality of that "smuggler"—and grounded in what Jean-Michel Rabaté calls "*logos skouriatikos*," embracing "the rationality of corrosion doubling as generation" (2018: 113)—thus belongs to plasticity; a concept that, stronger than the formless, shows the productive tension and dialectical conflict between forms and their generative distortions.

Formal Disturbances Are Grounded in the Affective Operations that Rewrite Form

If the plasticity of forms involves their creative capacity of transformation as well as a disruptive potential to "explode the form," a crucial question arises: What is this force that puts the forms into a disruptive motion, a force that invades the formal integrity, ontological stability, and wholeness, a force that ultimately puts forms at the very limits of representation? The answer that the second premise of this book proposes is that this force is affective and comes about not so much from the way these affects are felt, perceived, or experienced by the affected subject but rather from their capacity to act upon forms while opening them anew. In the wake of the recent scholarly work coming to terms with the affective turn that emerged in the mid-1990s and which has been spinning vividly across all humanities and social sciences until now, a proper outline of its various strands and their subsequent recurrent critique would go well beyond the scope of this introduction. Instead of paraphrasing the key definitions and the usual genealogy of the term, it seems useful to make a choice from the emergent scholarship and to open a dialogue between two approaches advocated by some of the leading voices of the contemporary cultural affect theory that build upon the concepts of relational and formal affect.[8] Without holding the same methodological positions, these voices often overlap with each other by making a decisive step from affect as an *expression* of and an *effect* on the affected subject to the *agency* of affects and their performativity. Let us begin with a remarkably sharp, polemic, and particularly compelling voice of the film scholar Eugenie Brinkema, whose position of affective formalism can be best adumbrated contra its conceptual adversaries.

Despite the considerable impact of the affective turn on the humanities, the notion of affect in aesthetic forms and cultural objects has become constricted by its understanding as either a matter of bodily sensations or an emotional interiority, escaping representation and meaning, and determined to be *felt* rather than scrutinized. Although the former view builds upon Spinozan-Deleuzian terms elaborated by Brian Massumi, who famously defined affect as a virtual and autonomous corporeal *intensity* that is "unqualified," "not ownable or recognizable" and "thus resistant to critique" (2002: 28), it comes down to the same theoretical problem as the latter which posits affect as a certain je ne sais quoi beyond signification.[9] Furthermore, such a view reveals a paradox, one that comes about as a persistent blind spot of affect theory in general; despite Deleuze's and Guattari's insistence that "pure affects imply an enterprise of desubjectification" (2004: 297), they are often described in terms of an intentional entity aimed at a perceiving subject, as a kind of phenomenal force moving— that is, "doing something affective to"—the subject. While this position articulates affect in terms of embodiment and sensation, as a visceral, immediate experience, and an irrational, nonsignifying, and unstructured force, Brinkema—who dubs this Deleuzian tendency ironically "a repetition with no difference" (2014: xiii)—proposes to end up with the vague vocabulary of the ineffable intensities and instead to attend to the formal activity of specific affects. Denouncing prevailing approaches in affect theory for completely disregarding textuality and close reading in favor of privileging the affected subject with its personal feelings and sensations, Brinkema contends: "If affect as a conceptual area of inquiry is to have the radical potential to open up ethical, political, and aesthetic avenues for theoretical inquiry, then, quite simply, we have to do better than documenting the stirrings of the skin" (2014: 37–8).

However, rather than the "enjoyable audacity of its attack on contemporary film studies," as one of the reviewers of Brinkema's *The Forms of the Affects* phrased the book's polemical drive (Hanich 2015: 112), what this book elaborates upon is Brinkema's central argument that affects which are always plural and differ one from another *have* forms: in the sense of specific and unique aesthetic structures that must be *read for*. Unlike the common identification of affect with the intentional expression and bodily sensation *for* the spectator, a sensation that is, once again, allegedly anti-representational, ineffable, and beyond any signification, she turns her attention from interiority of the classical subject, replete with emotions and feelings, to both the aesthetic and speculative work of forms and argues for the concept of *formal affect* which explains any affect as a desubjectifying "self-folding exteriority that manifests in, as, and with textual form" (2014: 25). Reading closely cinematic forms, such as light, color, rhythm, and duration, but also montage and mise-en-scène, leads to the crucial observation that "affective force works over form, that forms are auto-affectively charged, and that affects take shape in the details of specific visual forms and temporal structures" (2014: 37). What she calls the "radical formalism" has thus a great potential for the following mediaphilosophical inquiry in that it helps to examine the formal work and mediality of affects—in their capacity to disrupt and transform aesthetic forms. Attending to Brinkema's emphasis on the speculative force of forms and affects, this book, however, takes a slightly different turn since its starting points are not particular forms of affects—such as disgust, joy, grief, or horror—and their cinematic structures but rather the encounters with the disturbances *to* form, collisions that drive and are, in turn, driven by affective operations.

Undoubtedly, Brinkema is not the only theorist who has her share in dismantling the subjectivist baggage of the ongoing affective turn. The second cluster of voices belongs to the relational approach as advocated by such scholars as the visual theorist Ernst van Alphen and the philosopher Jan Slaby, whose common ground lies in the shift from the ontological questions relating to the expression of the subject's inner self to the performative processes, mediations, and situations within which subjects are constituted, connected, and mutually conditioned through affective agency. While Slaby explains the notion of affect as "a relational dynamic between individuals and in situations—a dynamic that is prior to individual experience" (2019a: 60), van Alphen proposes affects as intensities triggered by an encounter with unconventional forms that "shock to thought" (2019: 163). What makes their relational concepts especially useful for an affective reading is that they restore the foundational *two-way movement* of affect involving the forces of bodies and objects of affecting and being affected, as defined by the major predecessor of the affective turn Baruch Spinoza in his *Ethics* (1677), through the opposition between *affectus* and *affectio*, usually translated as affect and affection. If the former signifies the force whereby "the body's power of acting is increased or diminished, aided or restrained" (Spinoza 1994: 154), the latter stands for the "state of a body insofar as it suffers the action of another body" (Deleuze 1997: 138). Rather than discarding the question of the subject altogether—and thus falling into the trap of what Graham Harman calls "taxonomic fallacy" of relational approaches (2012: 192)[10]—the affect scholars in question make a more nuanced theoretical move by positioning the subject's agency, roles, and performances within connections to other subjects, objects, and events.[11]

In his pathbreaking synthesis of the two then dominant strands of affect theory—roughly, the philosophical-aesthetic which mainly draws on Deleuzian-Guattarian reading of Spinoza, and the psychobiological, inspired by the work of Silvan Tomkins and his followers Eve Kosofsky Sedgwick, Adam Frank, and Teresa Brennan—van Alphen argues for the concept of *affective operations*, based on the assumption of agency and affective *transmissions* of matter and objects. Within these parameters, affects function as Deleuzian "energetic intensities," which precede and exceed the signification and a given meaning but, crucially, "are always the result of an interaction between a work and its beholder" (van Alphen 2008: 26). In order to unpack the theoretical possibilities of van Alphen's operational notion of affects—a notion that allows an analytical inquiry into what precisely affects *do* and how they *operate*—it is important to note their twofold condition. For one thing, the transmission of affect stands always for a social process taking place between subjects and cultural objects; for another, the process of affective transmission excludes any causality between a transmitted affect and both the individual content and emotional "charge" that the affected subject can ascribe to it. As such, the transmitted affect can be given content and "feel like depression, anger, or anxiety. But the way a transmitted affect is signified differs from person to person. [. . .] The same affect can evoke very different feelings or thoughts in different people" (2008: 25).

Now, since van Alphen joins Deleuze's assertion that affect "produces feelings and emotions" while also catalyzing a "shock to thought" (2008: 22, 24), it comes as no surprise that he proposes the term of operations which results from the cultural objects' affective agency, that is their capacity to transmit affects throughout their particular textual or visual structure to a reader or a viewer. Surprisingly, however, he gives only two concrete examples of these operations—powerful visual descriptions and the psychic process of identification (2008: 27–9)—which belong, I would object, among traditional instances of the usual representational reading rather than doing justice to his capacious operational term. Taking the bait of van Alphen's compelling proposition that "the affective operations and the way they shock to thought are what opens a space for the not yet known" (2008: 30), the following chapters will offer their own operations of *shattering, saturating, revaluating,* and *shifting,* which pursue the desubjectifying logic of the relational approach and thereby deontologize affects in favor of emphasizing their performative qualities. For to grasp the conceptual gains of the affective operations that always come up when "the affective trigger is pulled" (van Alphen and Jirsa 2019: 8), it seems necessary to link them with and situate within the specific media sites wherein the performativity of affects emerges. And these sites lie nowhere else than within the fabric shaped by an incessant work of forms.

To conclude, whereas Brinkema localizes affects at the level of form, composition, and structure while reading them beyond narrative thematic and moral symbolism, van Alphen holds the relational position grounded in the idea of affective interaction between a performative agency of an object and the viewer-reader. Although it may seem that Brinkema's radical formalism excluding affect from the matter of expression and spectator's sensation stands in direct opposition to van Alphen's relational view, one of the ambitions of this book is to reconcile both approaches which are, in fact, complementary. Because even though the encounters with the often shocking, frustrating, or fascinating disturbances to form that the present inquiry traces do produce an affect in terms of what Brinkema, in a playful wink to Deleuze, phrases as "a *repli* that does not reply" (2014: 36), this affective *repli,* as I will argue, is *deployed* in its mediality. As such, any affect works as a *fold* that does *unfold*—both within the aesthetic forms and upon their beholder. Where, how, and to what extent this operational process of unfolding takes place and what that means for affective analysis and media theory will be the main address of the following chapters.

By focusing on the particular twofold moments during which the literary, the visual, and the audiovisual forms engender affects, and when these affects disrupt and reshape the already established forms again, the conceptual thrust of *Disformations* is to shed light not only on the formal work of affects but also on the affective work of forms. By no means does this double emphasis call for a comeback to an individual affected reader or a spectator; rather, it is an attempt to observe the two-way movement of affects in between the force of *affectus* and the traces of *affectio*, that is in their performative mediality produced by and within texts, images, and sounds. Instead of turning artworks into "containers for the psychology of the spectator" (Adorno 2002: 275), this book pays attention to those spectators only insofar as they take part in the affective operations generated by the work of forms—as a body, as the subject, or any other form as such.

Aesthetic Forms Think with and through Intermedia Figures

This takes us to the third premise of this book, which is that aesthetic forms do the work of thinking *through* and *with figures* that pervade genres, authorial styles, and contextual boundaries of literature and arts. Holding to this premise in the following chapters, I argue that inasmuch as the performative force of affects needs to be thought relationally, the aesthetic forms and cultural objects should be considered *intermedially*; that is, across their generic boundaries and in their essential hybridity, which does not, nevertheless, prevent us from attending to their specificities, differences, and singularities.[12] To do so, the main analytical emphasis will be put on concrete intermedia figures in their aesthetic rearrangements and transhistorical movement across literary and audiovisual media. Although the major concern of this book is the affectively driven generative deformations as rendered by modern literary texts, it shifts the attention from the representational, cognitive, political, and narrative regimes of the texts—or any other master signifying system whose unearthing prevails in the current literary studies—to their performative mechanisms, intermedia relations, and affective operations, and hence to the qualities and processes that are best explained in dialogue, confrontation, or even clash with other discursive and nondiscursive forms. Instead of using literature in its permanent negotiation with other arts to demonstrate, exemplify, or illustrate values, convictions, and narrative patterns that we already knew in advance, the critical claim of *Disformations* is that only through linking the disturbances to form with the affective agency can we learn something new about the aesthetic and theoretical force of media.

Subscribing to the famed first axiom of the so-called German media theory, announced by Lorenz Engell and Joseph Vogl in their forward to *Kursbuch Medienkultur* (Media Culture Handbook, 1999), that "there are no media, at least not media in a substantial and historically stable sense" (Herzogenrath, ed. 2015: 1) and that media exceed their material supports, symbolic systems, and techniques of distribution (Engell and Vogl, 2002: 10), the notion of medium as used in this book is anything but given, clearly defined, and ontologically stable object dwelling in the communication model based on more or less reliable conveying of a preexisting message. Therefore, the present discussion joins the theoretical positions of those contemporary literary, visual, and mediaphilosophical scholars who move away from seeing media as mere tools for the transmission of meaning and representation of a pre-established content to rather examine them as dynamic interfaces that "activate[s] our senses, our reflexivity, and our practices" (Casetti 2015: 5) while allowing to understand various processes, events, and transformations of their aesthetic performances.

To elaborate upon this mediaphilosophical gist and to show how the aesthetic forms produce their own figural thinking, but also how these figures invite us to rethink the borderlands between discursive and nondiscursive, this book undertakes a close reading of the following intermedia figures that exceed their contextual frames and generic boundaries stretched out between rococo engravings, modernist fictions, contemporary video art, and posthuman visual experiments: the faceless face, the wallpaper pattern, the garbage dump, and the empty chair. Performing the unsettling labor of *disformation* while pushing the recognizable forms to the limits of representation, the works of writers and artists, including Vincent van Gogh, Charlotte Perkins Gilman, Gaston Leroux, Richard Weiner, Ingmar Bergman, Michel Tournier, Francis Bacon, Eugène Ionesco, Vladimir Nabokov, Michal Pěchouček, Joseph Kosuth, Jan Šerých, among others, open up an avenue for addressing the affective operations that are not just aesthetically but also theoretically generative. But since the book's major strategy is thinking through and with the figures of *disformations* to shed light on both the formal work of affects and the affective work of forms, the very term "figure" deserves a brief explanation.

To plead for the theoretical force of aesthetic figures is hardly original and one could easily outline a genealogy of figural thinking comprising such disparate scholars as Auerbach (1938/1984), Lyotard (1971/2011), Deleuze (1981/2005), Barthes (1977/2002), Didi-Huberman (1990/2005), W. J. T. Mitchell (1994), Aumont (1996), D. N. Rodowick (2001), and J. H. Miller (2012), at some of whose concepts the following chapters will take a closer look. When pondering the essential heterogeneity of both visual and verbal representation as well as the porousness of their media boundaries, Mitchell coins a neologism of "the image/text" that functions as "neither a method nor a guarantee of historical discovery" but "more like an aperture or cleavage in representation, a place where history might slip through the cracks," and concludes that this notion can best be described as a "*theoretical figure*": "a site of dialectical tension, slippage and transformation" (1994: 104, 106). In a surprisingly Barthesian vocabulary, Mitchell proposes a fruitful albeit somewhat under-elaborated concept invested in the epistemological drive of thinking with texts and images, one that soon finds its echo in the aforementioned Aumont's observation—from the book with the telling title *À quoi pensent les films* (What Do Films Think About, 1996)—that "image thinks through figures, if we accept to fill the term figure with all the density of history that is much more than etymology" (1996: 170). However, whereas Mitchell's theoretical figure is primarily a scene of encounter between iconology and ideology, what I instead propose is to lodge such figures not only with certain thoughts, ideas, and views, grounded in various media representations, but also with the affective agency that drives their formal work and structures their aesthetic space.

Such is also a lesson of Lyotard's *Discourse, Figure* (1971), introducing the concept of *figure* as "a spatial manifestation that linguistic space cannot incorporate without being shaken, an exteriority it cannot interiorize as *signification*"—although embedded in language—and as "a violation of discursive order" (2011: 7, 268)—although making part of it. Rather than a stable and distinctively represented object, the figure thus embraces a force of the formal disruption which is poised *spatially* in between the discursive and the visual fields, without bounding their spatial and temporal regimes, as Rodowick points out, to the logic of binary oppositions (2001: 46).[13] Lyotard's intermedia stance is taken up by Bertrand Gervais and Audrey Lemieux who situate the concept of the figure at the junction of the readable and the visible while approaching it in a broad sense of "a dynamic sign which has the instability of the imaginary," which "can also serve as an *interface* and *a relay*, it incites and brings about reactions and discourses, it includes the affectivity of the subject who approaches it" (2012: 1; emphasis added). Despite perhaps too many meanings than one concept could meaningfully accommodate, what seems especially useful for this book's attempt to think with the intermedia figures is the emphasis here on the figural *mediality* which exceeds any idea of a fixed and clearly defined media carrier.

Figures in this book—the aesthetic and theoretical objects in motion, that is—are made of various texts, images, and concepts and travel across different poetics, historical framings, and cultural boundaries. Consequently, they come close to what Hans Belting sees as the crux of the transhistorical nature of images that "are not confined by their historical, medial, and technical contexts" (2011: 36). As the four analytical chapters of this book demonstrate, the theoretical potential of these transhistorical and intermedia figures is to be unpacked from within their survivals, travels, and unexpected appearances across different times and diverse places. While such figures make possible the encounter of the readable and the visual, the discursive and the nondiscursive and constitute the sites of both the aesthetic and conceptual production, *thinking with the figures* by means of their close reading is, I want to suggest, better attuned to the arts' affectively driven performative mechanisms than an analysis of the artworks in their intentional totality.

While the following chapters speak clearly with one another and their topics, theoretical concerns, and arguments resonate between and among them, there is a rationale for their ordering. This arrangement follows the encounters with the four intermedia figures—the faceless face, the wallpaper pattern, the garbage dump, and the empty chair—which establish the sites of *disformations* structured around the affective operations of shattering, saturating, revaluating, and shifting that these figures respectively trigger. Insofar as these figures interrogate the affective agency of forms, the chapters are arranged according to the degree of explicitness with which the scrutinized artworks articulate the link between affects and generative deformations. The first chapter follows the most evident and crude variant of the affective work of disformation against the backdrop of the historical facial disfigurements and modernist faceless images that *shatter* the formal integrity of the face; the second chapter sets on a transhistorical journey of the wallpaper ornaments between the rococo engravings and the contemporary video art, a travel that manifests a *saturating* of forms through a subversive ornamental movement; and the third chapter engages in the *revaluating* of form through a close reading of the performative and speculative force of the garbage dump. To round off this avenue of disformations whereupon the human body will have been continually dispersing, fading, and disappearing, the fourth chapter investigates the affective operation of *shifting* through an enigmatic present absence seated at the empty chairs.

What happens when a face begins to lose its familiar form, falls apart, becomes faceless? And how can language mediate the barely thinkable experience of the gaze facing the formless? To answer these questions, Chapter 1 delves into the formal work and affective agency generated by several encounters between subjects and disfigured faces that took place during the second decade of the twentieth century. Reading the faceless images in modernist texts by Rainer Maria Rilke, Gaston Leroux, and Richard Weiner in dialogue with the war experiences of the *gueules cassées* (broken faces), the survivors of the First World War who suffered extensive facial injuries, as rendered by Bernard Lafont and Henriette Rémi, I argue that rather than simply represented the faceless faces are performed through the formal work of affects that structure their discursive forms. Not only do the witness accounts from the battlefront and the literary fictions share an emotional force of the traumatic images but they also enable affects of shock, disgust, and fascination to unfold and shape the texture of these faceless encounters. Shifting from an ontology of the face toward the formal analysis of the faceless encounters, the aim of this chapter is to demonstrate that far from merely providing a narrative theme or a striking visual motif, the faceless face operates as a figure that embraces, on the one hand, the aesthetics of the formless, and, on the other, the experience of the real.

While Chapter 1 is primarily concerned with the work of disformation in literary modernism, the task of Chapter 2 is to enquire a transhistorical figure of ornament whose affective force engenders not only formal disturbances and subversive formations across various wallpaper patterns in literature and arts but also a conceptual field for rethinking the relationship between the subject and a seemingly passive ornamental space. Investigating a cluster of literary and scholarly writings and moving images including the novel *Pnin* (1957) by Vladimir Nabokov, an autobiographical account of the historian Frank Ankersmit, Ingmar Bergman's film *Through a Glass Darkly* (1961), Charlotte Perkins Gilman's short story "The Yellow Wall-Paper" (1892), and the works of two contemporary Czech visual artists Michal Pěchouček (2004) and Jan Šerých (2005), the second chapter makes a case that wallpaper floral and geometric patterns stretching across the walls of interiors are anything but an innocent decoration and instead radically transform the human figures in their proximity while reconfiguring the surrounding space through the affective operation of saturating. Through an examination of the formal metamorphoses of the ornamental patterns that trigger the affects of fascination, confusion, and fear, while often bordering with madness, and the ways their forms are saturated by the excess of visual or textual detail, I argue that the wallpaper disformations manifest a scene of the transhistorical survival of the rococo ornamental curves and reiteration of a radical event that they brought about, one of the broken frame.

Chapter 3 takes us on a garbage dump. Specifically, it situates the inquiry into the affective and conceptual affordances of aesthetic forms onto the trash heap in Michel Tournier's 1975 novel *Gemini*, a text that can be read as a love letter to the once useful and then rejected forms that now strike back. While the diegetic garbage dump plays a pivotal role of the archaeological site where the main protagonist undertakes a hermeneutic of the collapsing civilization before and during the Second World War through the human refuse, the novel revaluates the garbage forms by ultimately transforming the degraded waste material into a performative configuration that lays ground for a novel media-theoretical concept that I will propose to call "diatext." By focusing on the encounter between the human subject and the garbage dump in their mutual mediality, this chapter explores how the affective operation of revaluating can turn a degraded material that seems good for nothing into a structure of the performative thinking. Rather than analyzing the ways in which various waste products are represented as distinctive narrative objects, which is a dominant approach of the current literary waste studies, this chapter explores what kind of media operations and performative mechanisms drive the revaluation of garbage, what garbage does within the formal work of the text, and how it forces us to think its aporetic logic whereby the human is no more a producer of trash but rather a medium of its material, performative, and epistemic force.

Is it possible to capture an absence of the human subject by means of a portrait? This question is addressed in Chapter 4 that follows a figure of the empty chair which embodies, mediates, and materializes the absent subject across the literary and visual works of Vincent van Gogh, Richard Weiner, Eugène Ionesco, Joseph Kosuth, and Hermann Bigelmayr to argue for a seemingly paradoxical concept of the "portrait of absence." Based on the operation of shifting and inspired by recent nonmimetic approaches to the portrait, this concept embraces an aporetic bind between a mediation of the subject and its physical non-presence. Taking its cue from Weiner's short story "The Empty Chair: Analysis of an Unwritten Short Story" (1916), which is based on a nuanced contradiction between what the text *says* and what it *does* and pre-echoes the founding work of conceptual art, Kosuth's *One and Three Chairs* (1965), the chapter looks at van Gogh's metonymical (self-)portraits of empty chairs, Ionesco's play *The Chairs* (1952), and Bigelmayr's sculpture *Lehrstuhl—leerer Stuhl* (2005). Probing the formal work of the affects of loss, expectation, and desire, this chapter demonstrates how the empty chairs, grounded in the logic of disformation by shifting the subject into its invisibility, reinscribe the affective presence into the bodily absence on the way to reconsidering what an emptiness can really mean.

Instead of a traditional conclusion, the final coda reopens the initial question: What happens when forms fall apart and what is the conceptual payoff in thinking intermedia relations through the agency of affects? Revisiting some of the voices of the current media philosophy and engaging them in a dialogue with cultural affect studies, this last chapter considers the relationship between the operational qualities of affects and the material basis of the aesthetic media to argue for a direct link between an affective interaction and a media excess. For it seems that due to the tendency of affects toward accumulation, combining, and intertwining, notwithstanding the affects that can appear contradictory to each other, media have a capacity to exceed their material, generic, and semantic boundaries. In other words, the affective interaction, grounded in both their formal and relational qualities, generates a media excess through which individual discursive and nondiscursive forms transform their aesthetic ontologies. Such a media excess—the "intermedia surplus" as it were—is to be found during the moments when and at the sites where a text ceases to be a mere discursive structure, an image acquires other than purely visible qualities, and a sound overcomes its uniquely aural condition, thus amplifying the hybrid movement of forms which simply do not care about their aesthetic purity. The mediaphilosophical potential of affective operations thus reveals something that other disciplines are usually reluctant to cope with: an essential instability of their own object.

If, as Brinkema concludes her vigorous plaidoyer for form, "[t]aking forms and affects as mutually consequent, reading for their shaping of each other, instructs us in a lesson about the possibility for the new, the not-yet vitality of both form and affectivity" (2014: 261), let us begin this book with a hope not only that the double bind of forms and affects will be justified through the following close readings of the affective operations that arise from the specific aesthetic structures and from their own figural ways of thinking but that these particular operations are also general enough to allow a further use in our thinking with media.

Chapter 1

FACING THE FACELESS

MODERNISM, WAR, AND THE WORK OF DISFIGURATION

> What I want to do is to distort the thing far beyond the appearance, but in the distortion to bring it back to a recording of the appearance.
>
> David Sylvester, *The Brutality of Fact: Interviews with Francis Bacon*, 1975

On November 27, 2005, an important milestone in the history of the face took place when the first partial facial transplant was performed at Amiens University Hospital in France. During the fifteen-hour-long operation, a team of surgeons led by Bernard Devauchelle transplanted the nose, lips, chin, and cheeks from a brain-dead donor to a 38-year-old French woman whose face had been mauled by her dog after falling into a deep sleep induced by an overdose of sleeping pills. Although both the accident and operation attracted a high level of media coverage and intense scholarly interest, surprisingly little attention was paid to the testimony of the beneficiary of the transplant, Isabelle Dinoire.[1] In an interview for *Le Monde* in July 2007, eighteen months after the successful operation, the patient described her condition shortly before the transplant: "I couldn't breathe through my nose because there was nothing left. I had slipped into another world. I didn't dare leave my room. I couldn't bring myself to look at myself, but to impose that on others . . . . It was monstrous, traumatic, unpresentable. Standing in front of the mirror, I felt as if there was nothing of me left" (Cojean 2007: 20). Apart from the unimaginable amount of suffering the patient had to undergo, the absence of complete relief in wake of the operation, not to mention the self-alienating experience of confronting a new self, what is most striking about her comments is the language used to describe the transformation of what is the most exposed part of a person's identity into a horrifying uncanny object, one that must henceforth strive to make its "unpresentable" appearance presentable. The difficulty of rendering the unspeakable experience of facial disfigurement into discourse seems to have been overcome by a sudden switch whereby the individual self had become an objectified "it."

In his study on the affective capacity of the face, the pioneer of psychobiological theory Silvan Tomkins made a significant equation between the human being and the face, defining the latter as the primary site of affects (1995: 263). Considering the dreadful experience of losing one's face, this raises some pertinent questions: What happens when the face begins to lose its familiar form, falls apart, and becomes faceless? If the face is no longer a guarantee of identity or a reliable sign of interiority but instead an unrecognizable, nameless, and disturbing object, what kind of affects do these shattered faces trigger and how do such affects operate? And how can language mediate the barely thinkable experience of the gaze facing the faceless? Rather than contributing to the history of representation of facial disfigurement or parsing the emotional responses this phenomenon brings about, this chapter delves into the formal work and affective agency generated by several encounters between subjects and disfigured, erased, or simply faceless faces that took place during the second decade of the twentieth century. Reading the faceless images in several modernist texts by Rainer Maria Rilke, Gaston Leroux, and Richard Weiner in dialogue with the war experiences of the *gueules cassées* (broken faces), the survivors of the First World War who suffered extensive facial injuries, as rendered in the novel *Au ciel de Verdun* (The Skies Over Verdun, 1918) by Bernard Lafont and the war memoirs *Hommes sans visage* (Men Without Faces, 1942) of the Swiss front nurse Henriette Rémi, I will argue that rather than simply represented the hardly thinkable faceless faces are *performed* through the formal work of affects that structure their discursive forms.

Not only do the witness accounts from the battlefront and the literary fictions share an emotional force of the traumatic images but they also enable affects of shock, fear, disgust, and fascination to unfold and shape the texture of these faceless encounters. By revolving around the Lacanian *real*—a constitutional failure of reality suffused with trauma, shock, and pain, a "crack within the symbolic network itself" (Žižek 2008b: 215)—the texts dealing with disfiguration perform this crack through the affective operation of *shattering* that comes about as a result of the fearful encounter with the faceless and allows to think of the face as a site of formal conflicts rather than a place of identification. Shifting from an emotional ontology of the face toward the affective analysis of the faceless encounters, the following lines will also demonstrate that far from merely providing a narrative theme or a striking visual motif encompassing the imagery of horror, disgust, and fascination—as employed widely in expressionist literature and visual arts but also in horror and sci-fi cinema—the faceless operates as a figure that embraces, on the one hand, the aesthetics of the formless and, on the other, the traumatizing experience of war.[2] The disturbances, shattering, and "formlessnessing" of the formal integrity of the face will be explored in conversation with both the relational and formalist approaches to affect, a conceptual encounter that helps to understand how the affective force of the faceless not only works "over form" (Brinkema 2014: 37) but also triggers latent experiences in all those who face it.

To keep up with the conceptual premise of this book arguing that rather than an artistic destruction, an intentional elimination, or ontological negation of form, *disformations* stand for the affective operations that open the form toward new formations and disturbances, and that such deformations situating form at the very limits of representation are both aesthetically and theoretically generative, it is important to carefully trace how this unsettling agency of affects penetrates into the texture of media and drives their forms, whether rooted in modernist literary discourse or witness accounts from the battlefront. One of these representational limits that the language nonetheless strives to name and perform emerges when a human face—the proverbial "pathway to the soul"—is turned inside out.

Shattering the Face in Modernism

Shortly before and after the First World War, literary modernism began to abound in the uncanny images of the faceless face. In a fragment from the beginning of Rilke's only novel, *The Notebooks of Malte Laurids Brigge* (1910), an initially melancholic scene involving an anonymous poor woman on a Parisian street quickly morphs into a terrifying event.

The woman sat up, frightened, she pulled out of herself, too quickly, too violently, so that her face was left in her two hands. I could see it lying there: its hollow form. It cost me an indescribable effort to stay with those two hands, not to look at what had been torn out of them. I shuddered to see a face from the inside, but I was much more afraid of that bare flayed head waiting there, faceless [*bloßen wunden Kopf ohne Gesicht*]. (1990: 7; 2012: 12)

Far from simply depicting a shocking inversion of the face, faithfully echoing the traumatic dimension of the anonymous life in modern metropolis, the scene displays a complex transgression of the gaze. The laconically described, chillingly dreadful situation of facial removal stands for a moment during which the anthropological order is violated while staging the encounter of the subject with the uncanny object.[3] The inside of a face, embodying, as aptly noted by Gerhard Richter, "the unthinkable inside of something that is the very definition of the outside" (2012: 113), suddenly changes from the observed object to a space entered by the frightened narrator from whose perspective the whole scene is focalized. This perspective is then doubled as the narrator struggles between, on the one hand, the inquiring surgeon-like gaze at what Malte's eyes cannot avoid—the reverse of a face, the hollow skin clutched in the palms—and, on the other, the voyeuristic and terrified gaze, eager to see—while taming the desire to do so—the gaping remains of the bodily reversion, the faceless head.

As a result, two different regimes of *seeing* underpin the entire scene. While the narrator deals with his own fears, the text leads the reader to the place where Malte's eyes dare not look, to the faceless, disfigured head. And if the language remains descriptive and coherent, it is the *gaze* that is split—between both narrative modes of seeing and between what Rilke explicitly depicts and what his text allows us to get a glimpse of: an image that is not *visibly* represented but instead *visually* performed.[4] For when the female protagonist's face is torn off by her abrupt movement, another gaze, belonging neither to the narrator nor to the observed woman, enters the scene: the gaze of the groping reader watching the right and so far invisible side of the skin, the facial object peeping through her fingers. Along with the gaze, the transgression also disturbs the semiotics of the face whose etymology, rooted in the German word *Gesicht* and the French word *visage* (coming from the Latin word *visum* denoting both seeing and sight), links the viewed object to the very act of seeing while referring to the face as "something that we see in front of us and that in turn looks back at us" (Schmitt 2012: 7). Through the traumatic encounter with the faceless, Rilke—in "his farewell to the face," as Hans Belting recently dubbed the novel (2017: 23)—thus undertakes a double transgression of both the gaze and the anthropological meaning of the face, showing that the face from the inside is not just an affective site of fear and fascination but that these affects also *trigger* the split between two kinds of seeing—the representational and the performative one.

The same year saw the publication of Gaston Leroux's famous novel *The Phantom of the Opera* (1910). Erik, the novel's ghostlike protagonist, is a mysterious phantom with a disfigured face who lives in an underground labyrinth beneath the Paris Opera House. Described as a repulsive skeleton who wears a mask to conceal his monstrous noseless face, a glimpse of his eyes alone is enough to traumatize the viewer. Adopting a partly satiric and partly enigmatic tone, the narrator introduces "the most extraordinary and fantastic tragedy" (Leroux 2012: 5), teasing out the superstitions and ripe imaginations of both the diegetic characters and readers. Firmly rooted in the genre of the Gothic novel with its touch of the burlesque, the novel precisely evokes the equivocal nature of a lost soul dwelling at the very edge of a physical and fantastic existence.[5] As such, the verbal depiction of the disfigured face is preceded by a profound trace, or rather *cleavage*, in the memory as experienced by one of the protagonists who saw the monster just for one second and yet "the memory of what he had briefly glimpsed had left an indelible mark on his mind" (2012: 13). Echoing the unbearable recollection of the phantom, this traumatic pattern will recurrently appear throughout the whole text while competing with the actual sight of the phantom to such an extent that it will occasionally overshadow it.

For the cultural historian Sander L. Gilman, the mystery of Eric's disfigured face could not be clearer. In his view, the phantom's missing nose along with his fixed pupils and the stench of the rotten flesh functioned for a common reader at the turn of the century as an obvious indicator of social disease, evoking the hereditary physiognomy of syphilis. However persuasive Gilman's observation that "[a]ll lost noses, according to the common wisdoms of the nineteenth century, the age of syphilophobia, were signs of sin" (1998: 34) certainly is, it remains grounded in the physiognomic reading of the face as an external sign of the interior morality, and hence fails to account for the aesthetic work of the disfigured face affecting both the language and gaze of its beholders. From a different perspective, Žižek, in his psychoanalytic and joyfully intertextual reading, argues that the phantom's repulsive face stands for a site of an intrusion of the real: "*The amorphous distortion of the face*: the flesh has not yet assumed definite features; it dwells in a kind of preontological state, as if 'melted,' as if deformed by anamorphosis" (1991: 47). Rather than pursuing Žižek's anamorphic view that leads him to disclose the vibrant horror under the mask through specific ideological meanings, I want to take his argument one step further by suggesting that this amorphous distortion of the phantom's face comes about not as a lurking inherent potential to be yet accomplished but as a specific formal work of affects that are performed through the movement of language—that is to say, as an act of disformation.

No less conspicuous than the "palpitating skinned flesh" (Žižek 1991: 47) concealed beneath the mask are the phantom's eyes whose demonic force consists paradoxically in the contrast between presence and absence. "His eyes are so deep-set you can't hardly make out the pupils which never move. In fact, all you can see is two great big black holes like sockets in a dead man's skull" (Leroux 2012: 13). But the almost missing eyes—the holes that lead toward nothing else than to the groping trajectory of a look attempting to discern them, and hence to their confusing mediation by the text—do substitute and eventually overcome their partial absence by the effect of the mesmerizing gaze; in fact, they lead to the "eyes popping out" (2012: 14) of the bystander's head, making the sight of the phantom no easier to countenance. As if the negative sentence uttered by Erik were addressed not only to the opera singer Christina Daaé but also to the whole account of the novel's impossibility of representation: "You will never see Erik's face!" (136). Rather than translating the generative negativity of this paradoxically unseen and yet observed facial object into a physiognomic screen upon which the others' anxieties would have been projected, or, as Žižek suggests, reading the figure of phantom allegorically as "a *fetish* that stands in for the class struggle" (1991: 62),[6] the affective agency that emerges whenever the phantom's faceless face appears opens up a different theoretical avenue for thinking the formal disturbances. The necessary question then is: How can language capture, mediate, and perform such an experience of the unseen, shocking, and barely nameable face oscillating between presence and absence?

In his take against the traditional reduction of the face to a legible sign, Didi-Huberman argues for a notion of the "ruckus of the face" (*le chahut du visage*) that exceeds the borders of psychological and physiognomic expression and has "a capacity to open before us as a field, a source of agitation, conflicts, and symptoms" (1992: 44). To play out this desubjectifying and *loud* facial field, the linguistic means that Leroux employs involve an insisting accumulation of synonyms and repetitions, unveiling "a face so pale, so grim, so repulsive" (2012: 32). More importantly, anyone spotting Erik without his mask can only give voice to an overwhelming and purely affective speech—"Oh! Horror, horror, horror!"—only to be repeated by the surrounding nocturnal echoes modified ever so slightly to produce: "Horror! . . . Horror! . . . Horror!" (2012: 139). Far from the language voiding itself through such repetition, what it actually achieves here is an *imitation of the unspeakability* of the disfigured face. In doing so, the text switches into a different operational mode whose main goal is less a depiction of the fearsome face and the related evocation of disgust, fear, and panic—a mode that is rather invested in *production* of an affective portrait shaped by the visual and acoustic qualities of what is essentially nameless and formless:

> If I live to be a hundred, I shall never forget the inhuman scream he uttered, his howl of hellish pain and fury, while my eyes, round with horror, remained fixed on that ghastly . . . *thing* . . . and my mouth stayed open but no words came out of it [comme ma *bouche* qui ne se refermait pas et qui cependant ne criait plus]! (2012: 139)

On the one hand, the language expands a peculiarly violent mechanism that reduces the most human part of the body to a nameless—both alive and dead—*object*, a fascinating yet monstrous and rejected "abject"; on the other hand, the protagonist's vocabulary reaches the discursive limits of shock and horror.[7] It should be therefore noted that despite the remarkable quality of David Coward's translation, at this point the English version eludes the affective force of the mutual— *transmitted*, as it were—scream in the original, taming the mouth as a simply discursive apparatus instead of the sonic hole which is at stake here.[8] Not only is the medium of language affected by this horrifying encounter with the monster, but the pathology of the repulsive face is also physically imprinted into the observer's physiognomy. For as long as the open mouth of the horrified subject screams and howls, everything is quite in order, but if the face also remains in this utmost affected position afterward—sustaining and reinforcing the unsettling effect of such a *mute scream*—the whole physiognomy, whose respective parts mimic each other, is trapped in the claws of perversion and disrupted temporality.

Such is also a lesson that the late modern paintings of Francis Bacon, on which the analogous rejection of the causal and narrative logic is played out, teach us.[9] As he intriguingly explained with regard to his series of screaming popes in an interview with David Sylvester in 1966: "You could say that a scream is a horrific image; in fact, I wanted to paint the scream more than the horror" (1993: 48). Without falling into the trap of what Brinkema dubs the "intentional affect" (2014: 33)—the calculated emotional effect aimed at affecting the viewer—Bacon was well aware that the scream lacking a motive is not just affectively but also conceptually much stronger than just an emotional expression of a ready-made horror.[10] I argue that the same holds true for Leroux's novel. The encounter with the phantom's disfigured face, which gradually becomes un unnameable object, triggers the disruptive work of affects that shatters the formal integrity of the face on the way to shifting the visible horror toward the limits of visual and verbal representation.

Both Rilke's transgression of the face turned inside out and Leroux's affective language transforming the Gothic phantom into a terrifying facial object that cannot be named but only screamed, culminate in the short story "The Erased Face" (Smazaný obličej), drafted by the Czech writer Richard Weiner (1884–1937) during and published right after the First World War as a part of his short story collection *Škleb* (Grimace, 1919). The poet, journalist, and novelist Weiner, who was born into a bilingual Czech-German bourgeois Jewish family and spent the most of his writing life in Paris, had the firsthand experience from the Great War as he entered the military service at the Serbian front in 1914, where he suffered a neurasthenic breakdown which led to his discharge from the army. Shortly after his return to Prague in 1915, he wrote a collection of stories inspired by war and entitled *Lítice* (The Furies, 1916), which renders the psychological dramas of the soldiers balancing on the verge of death both on battlefields and in the hell of the trenches. Abounding in an extremely complicated syntax, shifting rhythmical patterns, and archaic diction and vocabulary, which gained him during his lifetime reputation of an "odd" and "enigmatic" literary outsider, Weiner is acknowledged as one of the major modernist Central European writers whose work is compared to Franz Kafka by many scholars.[11] Furthermore, exceeding by far his usual label of expressionist, Weiner's synthesis of European avant-garde experiments, self-reflexive discourse, and bold metafictional strategies allow to understand him as one of the predecessors of postmodernism.

If Andreas Huyssen dubbed Rilke's novel "one of the most powerful and haunting articulations of a crisis of subjectivity under the pressures of urban modernisation" (2015: 79), Weiner's "The Erased Face" exposes the modern subjectivity to a *shock* whose affinity with the traumatic war experience is striking: the shock of a disfigured phantom, lacking face, name, and origin.[12] The only feature that makes this "oval stub, without a nose, without a mouth, without ears, even without hair, reminiscent of the scheme of a painter's mannequin" (1996: 331) human is the constant presence of a pair of piercing eyes that haunt both the narrator and the reader. Throughout the story, the phantom takes on various forms, as does the ever self-commenting narrative voice, which struggles to capture the terrifying sight of the faceless face as well as its affective impact. Preceded by an extensive essayistic prologue that outlines a radical conception of the non-causal history of the "inexplicable switches" and "terrible points" which "determine the curve of life" (318–19, 321), Weiner's short story has a dramatic structure, divided into five chronologically ordered scenes, each staging the longed-for yet frightening encounter of the narrator with a strange phantasmatic gaze and the faceless phantom to whom it belongs.

The second encounter, during which the narrating protagonist's desire to look into these foreign and yet familiar eyes leads to the terrifying arrival of the erased face, is initially imbued with an atmosphere of domestic banality. Upon returning home from the theater, the narrator sits down to eat his cold dinner alone. Sinking into his armchair from where his look is drawn to the white painted door that leads to the stairway, all of a sudden he becomes overwhelmed by an unintentional drumming of his fingers, which turns in to a mimicking of the rhythm and tune of the second act of Mozart's *Don Giovanni* in which the dead commander appears on the scene.

> I can see eyes. Real, living eyes; that slightly jelly-like matter where, as we know, the human soul resides; *that is to say vision*. This time it is just the eyes and nothing but them. Actually . . . ! They are embedded in a head. But the head is nothing but a fleshy, oval stub, without a nose, without a mouth, without ears, even without hair, reminiscent of the scheme of a painter's mannequin. This *erased face*, with its motionless living eyes; that is too terrifying for the horror to become even more intense. (331)

Triggering the affects of horror and shock, this fleshy stub, lacking facial organs and skin, whose human nature is nevertheless manifested by the presence of eyes and whose name—the "erased face"—Weiner is quick to typographically emphasize, makes even the language stumble: "that is too terrifying for the horror to become even more intense." Whenever this frightening faceless head makes its appearance, the rhythm of the syntax abruptly changes, either accelerating in a staccato pattern or becoming scattered through bifurcated sentences. It is as though the text were reticent to address the faceless head directly. While struggling to articulate at least some response to this shocking encounter through repetition of the impersonal and heavily symptomatic pronoun, the language introduces the only possible attribute that can be given to the form disrupted from within—the *formless*: "And I had the feeling that *It* is related to something in the future and that I am going to meet It again.

It did not resemble anything. Indeed, it was completely formless and yet tangible; but I did not know. I did not know" (326). What happens here in the course of a few sentences is nothing less than a *media shift* from the representational regime to the performative work of disformation. For giving a name to the paradoxical "formless" not only entraps the textual capacity of representation and meaning but also releases the language's affective motion of shattering by switching in confusion as it does between the self and the unnameable object—between "I" and "it"—before becoming entangled, even paralyzed, by its repetitions. Without this disturbing movement of textual forms, the formless would waste its affective potential and run dry as a mere semantic nonsense.

Hardly by accident, Weiner was writing his short story at the same time Freud was working on his essay on *Das Unheimliche*.[13] Both published in 1919, they share an encounter with a disturbing foreign face as well as a fascination with the familiar, yet horrifyingly unfamiliar, gaze. Whereas in Weiner's case the uncanny comes about through the goggling eyes fixed on a faceless stub, Freud examines this affective phenomenon through the literary motif of gouged eye sockets from the 1816 short story "Sandman" by E. T. A. Hoffmann and against the backdrop of his personal experience of failing to recognize his own face in the mirror. "I could not doubt it. They were foreign eyes, yet those foreign eyes were telling me something familiar" (327), announces Weiner's protagonist in a striking, yet obviously unconscious, resonance with Freud's famous passage in which the psychoanalyst depicts how he glimpsed the mirror image of his own face in the compartment of a sleeping car, mistaking it for the foreign face of an intruding doppelgänger.

This historical and thematic coincidence should not, however, overshadow the important differences between the lack of formal affordances in the psychoanalytical case and their plethora in "The Erased Face." While Freud defines the uncanny as "that class of the frightening which leads back to what is known of old and long familiar" and which, upon returning, can seem disturbingly unfamiliar (1981: 220), in Weiner's writing the traumatic returns of the faceless face oscillating between the unknown and the disturbingly familiar correspond to a dialectic *between figuration and disfiguration*, between losing and regaining form. If we agree with Anneleen Masschelein that it is more productive to read Freud's essay as a "theoretical fiction" rather than a rigorous psychoanalytical study and that the notion of the uncanny "can only be described in terms of an effect/affect experienced by the reader" (2011: 120, 156), it might be suggested that Weiner's *formless*, which makes the language stumble, resembles nothing known and yet seems shockingly familiar, arises as a formal condition of the uncanny. Not only do Weiner's, Rilke's, and Leroux's literary fictions share the uncanny images of the disfigured face but, more importantly, instead of merely representing them, they also enable affects of shock, disgust, fear, and fascination to unfold, shape, and *shatter* their own discursive forms while transforming the frightening and hardly thinkable faceless images into a site where affects open form.

Toward the Affective Work of the Formless

The faceless images and their performative force rendered by Rilke, Leroux, and Weiner lead to the same conclusion Didi-Huberman makes in relation to the "beautiful rag," a faint reminder of the discarded white drapery in Nicolas Poussin's painting *The Triumph of Pan* (1636): "It is disturbing as far as the fate anthropomorphism is subjected to is concerned: the human form has actually dissipated from it" (2002: 24). Such a disfiguration, which underpins the preceding literary images as well as their linguistic means, cannot be considered without the notion of the "formless," a term employed by Weiner ten years before Georges Bataille turned it into a key concept of his subversive materialist philosophy in the revue *Documents*, under the entry of its regular section Critical Dictionary, entitled "Informe" (1929). While his central theorem posits that the "*formless* is not only an adjective having a given *meaning*, but a term that serves to bring things down in the world, generally requiring that each thing have its form," he finally concludes that "affirming that the universe resembles nothing and is only *formless* amounts to saying that the universe is something like a spider or spit" (Bataille 1985: 31).[14]

However, whereas Bataille's original term targeted nothing less than the reductive power of rationalist thinking, for the present discussion about the affective agency of aesthetic forms and their generative deformations, the afterlife of the term seems to have provided more fruitful meanings. Elaborating the notion of the formless as an epistemological gesture within the scope of general visual anthropology—an approach he dubs in the Nietzschean fashion the "gay visual science" (*le gai savoir visuel*)—Didi-Huberman (1995) argues for the formless as a dialectical process of the creative deformation of forms, whose permanent motion, proliferation, and metamorphosis occur on the boundary between the visible and the invisible, nameable and unnameable, present and absent, the known and the unknown. In spite of its lexical meaning, the "formless" in no way stands for a destructive elimination that would lead to an absence of form, its dissipation into a mushy amorphousness, or to a muddy abstraction, but rather for a symptomatic event that involves a disturbance of forms and their internal decomposition: the transgression, the perpetual deformation, and the violent "opening of the form" (1995: 21). The formless, which can be then defined as an intrusion of the unknown into form and its new refiguration, thus functions not only as an unsettling morphological process, imparting to any form "a force of the dissimilar" (Didi-Huberman 1995: 135; *le pouvoir même du dissemblable*), but also, since it always yields new and disturbing formations, as an affective operation grounded in the shattering of a wholeness, recognizability, and formal integrity.

But what does it mean that forms are being opened from within their dissimilar reverse and how can formal disturbances trigger an affective activity? Taking his cue from Freud's *The Interpretation of Dreams* (1900), and especially from his notion of "work" in terms of a process during which given visual and discursive forms are breached and transformed into different arrangements, Didi-Huberman redefines the formless as a *"work of forms"* (*un travail des formes*). Such a work is "equivalent to what would be the *labor* of birth or agony: an opening, a rip, a process of rupture putting something to death and, within this very negativity, inventing something *absolutely new*" (1995: 21)—and hence involves the formal generation through deformation. On another occasion, when exploring the Christian iconography of Quattrocento, Didi-Huberman proposes an anthropomorphic analogy to the formless—a *"disfiguration"* which stands for a creative violence committed upon the classic imitation of the body. Rather than rejecting figuration in the traditional sense of representation and imitation, the disfiguration complies with Freudian "figurability," one that consists in *"modifying figures,* and thus in carrying out the insistent work of a disfiguration in the visible" (2005: 209). Psychoanalytic approaches are particularly helpful here as demonstrated by other scholars who recently contributed to the theory of the formless, most prominently Malabou, Évelyne Grossman, and Fédida. Grossman associates directly the notion of the formless with Antonin Artaud's creative violence of disfiguration, emphasizing that the latter "is not a pure and simple annihilation of the figure. It inscribes itself into the incessant movement of negation that at once dissolves and opens the form, displaces it, puts it in suspense, animates it . . . in one word, it brings the form to life" (2002: 17). To make his case, Fédida develops the notion of the formless in relation to Bataille's readings of the cave paintings in Lascaux and Manet's portrait of *Olympia* as "setting the forms into motion" (*la mise en mouvement des formes*) and a production of the image that "does not forget the forms of representation that seem to be expelled out of its center" (2000: 18–19).

With this spatiotemporal aspects in mind, it can thus be concluded that the formless comes about as an *event of disrupted representation* that triggers such affects as shock, fascination, confusion, horror, and uncanny which, in turn, intrude upon, shatter, remake, transform, and reinvent the hitherto recognizable forms.[15] This very event and *labor* of disformation, positioning as it does the known and familiar forms on the very edges of recognition shows clearly that the event of the formless not only abounds in new forms but also functions as a generator of affective operations. When looking back at the affective processes triggered by the uncanny faceless images in Rilke, Leroux, and Weiner, the affects of shock, fear, fascination, and the uncanny thus appear not as mere emotional states expressing an interiority of the affected subjects but rather as both forming and deforming forces. Underlying the work of the formless, these affects produce not only emotional and physical reactions in the reader but also, more importantly, new, shattered, and thoroughly concrete forms.

Admittedly, European literary modernism around the First World War is not the only reservoir of images for lost, disfigured, and formless faces. When Rilke reveals the torn-off face stuck in his woman protagonist's palms, however, the general questions his text poses to the form is the same a viewer of Bacon's paintings is also compelled to ask: How to name a face without a face and what do we experience when facing the faceless? Such a critical inquiry has been recently undertaken by the psychoanalyst Sylvie Le Poulichet (2009), who demonstrates how feelings of loss over the erasure of a person's face torment many psychiatric patients suffering from depersonalization disorder. In a particular strand of the clinical psychoanalysis labeled "*clinique de l'informe*," the formless accounts for unconscious pathological processes related to fluctuating identity and resulting symptomatic formations, ranging from the temporary loss of perception of different bodily parts, including the face, to feelings of self-absorption or partial necrosis of the limbs. According to Le Poulichet, these symptoms do not lead to a permanent state but rather embrace the dynamic process of mental transformation, during which "one thing constantly changes into its opposite and confirmation becomes identical with denial" (2009: 11). When going through what she calls the "unconscious formlessness," patients frequently undergo an identification of anxiety, experiencing it as a disintegration of the self. Under these circumstances, an inspection of oneself in the mirror does not result in the self-confirmation of a familiar appearance but instead engenders the fear of seeing a face about to fall apart (31–2). But how can a face become formless?

All three texts by Rilke, Weiner, and Leroux show clearly that the threat of the face losing its forms arises from the fact that such disfigurations reveal something the subject was never intended to see. If the face, a center of the sensory receptors, a primary site of affects and the proverbial pathway to the soul, is being deformed and, as Deleuze and Guattari (2004) would put it, dismantled and "effaced" by a violent disclosure of its reverse side, both the gaze that observes such a shattered face and the language that attempts to name it experience the formless as an intrusion of the traumatic real.[16] To follow the psychoanalytic inflection one more time, it is worth noting that this very experience was described by Lacan in connection with Freud's famous dream of Irma's injection (1895):

> There's *a horrendous discovery here*, that of the flesh one never sees, the foundation of things, the other side of the head, of the face, the secretory glands *par excellence*, the flesh from which everything exudes, at the very heart of the mystery, the flesh in as much as it is suffering, is formless, in as much as its form in itself is something which provokes anxiety. Spectre of anxiety, identification of anxiety, the final revelation of you are this—*You are this, which is so far from you, this which is the ultimate formlessness*. (1988: 154–5)

Although Lacan makes no direct reference to Bataille in his commentary on Freud's dream, which "can see the reverse side of the face through the open mouth" (Fédida 2002: 56), the noun "formlessness" corresponds closely to his materialist thinking on the formless as a disturbing possibility of form; as a terrifying, anxious, and uncanny view on the reverse side of a familiar body part; as a latency of the human being. Seeing a disfigured, suffering flesh subjects the viewer to an appalling experience of the traumatic real, revealing the formless as a founding part of our identity. In this light, the face turned inside out embodies a paradoxical synecdoche for the whole, yet formless, self. No matter how this "formlessness" is identified with a state of anxiety and shaped by a dream, it bears out a more general, fairly disturbing aporia: within our form, we are at the same time ultimately *formless*.

Inflicting Wounds upon Language: Gueules Cassées

So far, I have discussed the faceless, disfigured, and formless faces from several perspectives: as a literary transgression of the semiotics of the face, as a psychopathological experience of the real, and as the uncanny manifestation of the affective work of the formless. Neither Bataille nor anyone after him considered the formless as a mere metaphor placidly dwelling in the realm of art. On the contrary, as Didi-Huberman noted, "in its long course, history teaches us that people could be transformed by other people into the formless drapery of flesh matter" (2002: 109). Indeed, the figure of the faceless face reached its apotheosis in the wake of the massive facial injuries suffered by the survivors of the First World War, a phenomenon especially relevant to Weiner who had seen the atrocities of the war with his own eyes.[17] Although this experience was not completely new, only during this time were faceless heads seen for the first time on such a massive scale.

With a comforting cynicism and a touch of collective solidarity, the French term *gueules cassées* (broken faces) was established among the facially wounded soldiers from the First World War who returned with mutilated faces and traumatic experiences from the battlefront.[18] Combining medical history with social anthropology, Sophie Delaporte (2004) follows the wounded veterans from the dramatic moment of leaving the battlefield through the long and complicated medical procedures they had to undergo before they were transported to the closest surgical department to their difficult return home. Along with a description of surgical interventions, problems related primarily to poor hygienic conditions in military hospitals, and the general inadequacy of medical equipment, she focuses of the procedures behind facial reconstruction, now considered one of the milestones in the development of both reconstructive and plastic surgery. In order to explain the psychological impact of the profoundly destructive facial injuries, Delaporte probes the first visual confrontation of wounded soldiers with themselves as well as their encounters with family and close friends followed by their more or less successful reintegration into postwar society. Not surprisingly, such a "return to the normal" brought with it great difficulties, seeing that the facially injured had to come to terms with the loss of an essential part of their identity and perhaps the most human part of their body—the *visa du visage*, as Jacques Prévert metaphorically called it (Delaporte 2004: 175). Language facing the reality of the disfigured veterans affirms, however, that when it comes to the traumatic real, metaphors can quickly and violently transform a suffering subject into an alienated object. While the contemporary press accounts, as observed by Marjorie Gehrhardt, often described the disfigured as "inhuman monsters, pitiable victims or superhuman heroes" (2015: 106), using apocalyptic and somewhat grotesque imagery to compare them to "gargoyles," the metaphors employed by those who survived were no less cruel—as exemplified by a certain Marcel G. Stenay who described one of his fellow hospital invalids as "a nameless thing, a monstrous heap of torn flesh" (Delaporte 2004: 143).

Such dreadful spectacles can hardly be better attested to than by those who witnessed them firsthand, namely the soldiers, voluntary aids, and medical staff who were left traumatized by the sight of smashed, disfigured, or completely missing faces. As Delaporte points out, it was the stretcher-bearers who were mostly subjected to the first contact, bearing the wounded from the battlefield in the dark so as not to become "sitting ducks" themselves. No matter how sufficiently they were instructed, nothing could have prepared them for what they had to face, as testified by the following account from Bernard Lafont's novel *Au ciel de Verdun: Notes d'un aviateur* (The Skies Over Verdun: A Pilot's Notes, 1918):

> He is dead. But the other one isn't. And that's a great pity. What! A single grenade splinter can inflict such a wound?! Oh, hide that hideous face, hide it. I'm averting my eyes but I've seen it and I'll never forget it, even if I were to live until hundred. I've seen a man who had a bleeding hole instead of a face. Without a nose, without a face, all that disappeared, except for a wide cavity at the end of which the organs of the pharynx were moving. Without eyes, just shreds of eyelids hanging in the void. Hide that mask of horror [. . .] and the other one, the one with a marten's profile who has lost his lower jaw, too. (1918: 10–11)

It is difficult to discuss these lines without risking an accusation of playing down such painful reality. Certainly, any verbal description pales in comparison to this immediate experience that fully confirms Elaine Scarry's observation that "[w]ar is relentless in taking for its own interior content the interior content of the wounded and open human body" (1987: 81). In her groundbreaking book on the iconography of pain and suffering, Susan Sontag vividly points out the insufficiency of discourse when confronted with the bare view of the contemporary witness: "The nightmare of suicidally lethal military engagement [. . .]—above all the daily slaughter in the trenches on the Western Front—seemed to many to have exceeded the capacity of words to describe" (2003: 25). While framing the bloody catalogue of despair, pain, and horror as recounted by witnesses to one of the most horrific episodes in human history as anything other than faithful testimony might appear as ethically unsound, just like any other experience, giving voice to the traumatic and unspeakable *real* imprints itself on the symbolical—and, as such, must also be necessarily shaped, mediated, and transformed, not to overcome what Scarry phrases as "the nonreferentiality of the hurt body" (1987: 121) but rather to *inflict this injury upon* and *to perform it within language.*

The language used to approach what is beyond description is nowhere close to a neutral signifier or to a simple representation of the experienced horror. Instead of operating in an illustrative manner, it strives to grasp the unwatchable faceless faces in a violent and, in point of fact, *stylized* way. Lafont's rhetorical figure of repetition completes a rapid parataxis, juxtaposing the surgeon-like description of the mutilated face with subjective expressions of a painful distress. Both verbal modalities finally overlap, intensifying their effect through the metaphorical "mask of horror," images of a crater gushing blood and ruthless comparisons to the animal. In other words, language mainly serves the work of the formless, violently releasing the force of the dissimilar before abruptly transforming resemblance to dissemblance and upending the recognizable face onto its unrecognizable reverse. This formless reverse of the shattered face, I want to argue, is hence informed by the dreadful disfiguration and triggers the affects of horror, shock, and disgust which perform this very shattering within the textual medium.

Excelling in peculiar stylization and metaphorical practice, the next witness account is a depiction of a disfigured soldier from *Hommes sans visage* (Men Without Faces, 1942), the war memoirs of a Swiss front nurse who published under the pseudonym Henriette Rémi: "The whole face looks like a freshly ploughed field; for the similarity to be complete, the suction tube goes through two holes that seem to have been artificially dug into this tormented soil" (1942: 43).[19] The somewhat odd material imagination underlies the language which, as it were, short-circuits representation in favor of capturing and unfolding the affective modality of perspective. Consequently, the sentence opens up the position of the viewer-reader whose anthropomorphic view is undermined not only by the faceless image but also by the ruthless and, quite surprisingly, self-commenting language.

In her memoirs, Rémi also gives voice to one of the young nurse volunteers, suddenly standing "face to face with . . . with the most gruesome thing I have ever seen! [. . .]. Twenty 'men with wounded faces,' twenty monsters, men who have almost nothing human left about them, bodies bearing the mutilated ruins of a face" (1942: 36). While the horror depicted relates to the sight of the wounds, it is amplified by the ever-present latency that the viewer herself could turn into something similar: "His jawless face comes closer to me. I step back and the terrible half of the face keeps getting closer to mine" (37). This takes us back to the function of the uncanny gaze in the foregoing literary images. In both cases, the horror of a possible "version" of one's body and the latent identification with a mutilated and unrecognizable face, involving the disfigured object as well as the affective site where our gaze meets the other's gaze, are at stake.[20] These faceless images thus belong to literature as much as they do to the real world; in both cases their essential part is a hardly thinkable and yet tangible affective work of the formless.

A "mask of horror," a "bleeding hole," a "monstrous heap of torn flesh"—needless to say, all these words can only evoke the atrocious experience of encountering the faceless. The shock produced by the sight of these scenes, be they real or fictional, quickly turns from the viewed to the viewer, shaking the anthropological assumptions regarding our solid human form. Face to face with these images, the viewer is overwhelmed with affects; deep compassion gives way to horror, physical repulsion, and disgust, or, eventually, to shame at one's own voyeurism. Occurring every time we observe the other's suffering, as noted by Sontag, "[i]n each instance, the gruesome invites us to be either spectators or cowards, unable to look" (2003: 42). Moreover, the beholder becomes frightened by the sight of the wounds and suffering of another, which, observed by the beholder's own frightened gaze, are turned inward to her or his body. To observe the suffering of others blends with a great fear concerning our own human form, the dread of the possibility that our face, too, might turn into a similar formless mass. We are thus subjected to the affective power of images which, as Jill Bennett suggests, "have the capacity to address the spectator's own bodily memory; to *touch* the viewer who *feels* rather than simply sees the event, drawn into image through a process of affect contagion" (2005: 36). Although the contours of the human face are violently deformed, mutilated, and transformed into a deep open wound, on the part of the beholder's bodily memory, they always assume the form of a human face. The faceless as a latency of the face actually stems from the same dialectical logic of the formless as a possibility of form.

Rewriting the Faceless Experience

Thinking the literary images of Rilke, Leroux, and Weiner with the discourse surrounding the "broken faces," the introductory suggestion of a mutual dependence between the formal and relational qualities of affects comes to the fore again. The overview of the witness accounts shows clearly that even the unpresentable, barely imaginable, and painfully thinkable suffering calls for *rewriting*. Whether the discourse of the faceless uses metaphorical practices, breaks off, stammers, frantically repeats, or simply shifts from the horror faced to the account experienced by a viewer, it is a far cry from being a mimetic description, a transparent representation, or a proper reproduction. Instead, through the affective work of the formless, which *structures* both literary images and their verbal matter, form itself acquires uncanny and painful qualities. Following Brinkema's claim that such a form "takes up the peculiarly painful suffering, gives it shape, weight, intensity, and force" (2014: 99), I want to propose that due to this unsettling work of literary forms the affective operation of shattering unfolds its performative qualities. For the horror to fright, for the pain to hurt, and for the shock to disturb, they first need to rip the language up and deform it toward new formations.

Only then the very form, disrupted and yet reconfigured, allows for the affective transmission between these faceless images and their beholders. In order for the affects to unfold in contact with the reader-spectator and to produce feelings and emotions as well as words, images, and thoughts, it is necessary that they *trigger* a potential experience—in this case, the experience of the faceless. The language of the *gueules cassées* does the same formal work as the one performed by the literary faceless images. It neither merely describes a shocking reality nor simply depicts beholder's emotions but, instead, *imitates* the affected modality of perspective, while performing the split between the observed wounds and the terrifying possibility that the viewers themselves might turn into something similar. I therefore argue that the relational affect, whose main capacity is transmission between cultural object and beholder, and the formal affect, one that "may fold back, rebound, recursively amplify" (Brinkema 2014: 24), are indivisible and complementary. Merging into and substantially shaping the encounter with disfiguration, they both take part in the affective operation of shattering and become activated upon the face becoming faceless.

To be sure, I am not suggesting that the dreadful inhuman face displayed by Weiner, who had firsthand experience from the front lines of the Great War, has anything to do with an eyewitness testimony of the real experience of the facially injured veterans. I also do not claim that the literary faceless images, grounded in the aesthetics of the formless and releasing the encounter with the uncanny, prefigure the real human tragedy as witnessed by hundreds of thousands of the wounded soldiers. What I do argue is that the faceless face embodies a figure of disformation that combines the traumatic historical experience of the facial wounds with the aesthetic imagination of the disfigured face as advocated by modernism and shaped by the work of the formless—a figure that helps to rethink what the face, continually thwarted by a possibility of releasing its reverse side, really does. This is perhaps best manifested in the late modern portraits of Bacon who approached the human figure, face, and appearance primarily through the techniques of deformation and to whom any other face but a torn, erased, or disjointed one would be out of the question. "What I want to do is to distort the thing far beyond the appearance, but in the distortion to bring it back to a recording of the appearance" (Sylvester 1993: 40). These words, sharply summing up the dialectic between figuration and disfiguration, would hardly be so chilling without the historical experience from which the faceless portraits are fashioned.

Chapter 2

CURVES THAT BREAK THE FRAME

ON THE RELENTLESS ABSORPTION OF THE WALLPAPER PATTERN

> Thus designs *à la grecque*, foliage for borders or on wallpaper, etc.,
> signify nothing by themselves: they do not represent anything, no
> object under a determinate concept, and are free beauties.
>
> Immanuel Kant, *Critique of the Power of Judgment*, 1790

After discussing the modernist figure of the faceless face as an
encounter between aesthetics of the formless and experience of the real,
this chapter probes a transhistorical figure of ornament whose affective
force produces not only novel subversive formations across various
wallpaper patterns in literature, the visual, and the audiovisual arts but
also a conceptual field for rethinking the relationship between subjects
and their allegedly passive space. To read a concept out of the aesthetic
work of forms requires one to take an artistic medium as a *theoretical
object* in its own right, one that, as Hubert Damisch puts it, generates
thinking in that it "obliges you to do theory but also furnishes you with
the means of doing it" (Bois et al. 1998: 8). This is where the notion of
figure is particularly helpful as it provides such a theoretical tool—a
kind of "limb" of its conceptual anatomy. While the preceding chapter
demonstrated how a specific figure of disformation is endowed with
cultural memory and acquires its aesthetic force through the affective
operation of shattering, in what follows I will look at how another figure,
materialized through a transhistorical motion of ornament, generates
peculiar *spatial* formations through the affective operation of saturating
triggered by fascination, confusion, and fear.

But how does an unsettling affective activity generating novel
formations relate to something so innocent, light-hearted, and
decorative as an ornament? Why should its spatial relations matter to
a mediaphilosophical inquiry, and what is at stake in rethinking the
ornament beyond the Kantian "free beauty" and rather as a disturbing

figure whose radical aesthetic potential cannot be thought without its permanent excess? To begin with the latter question, let's recall Lyotard's definition of figure as an unruly site of a semantic tremble, "a spatial manifestation that linguistic space cannot incorporate without being shaken" (2011: 13). The figure is, by its very definition, not only widely polysemous but also scholarly democratic. As *OED* tells us, the twenty-four lexical meanings of the word *figure* can be divided into five interrelated semantic categories: (1) form, shape; (2) represented form, image, likeness; (3) delineated or devised form, a design or pattern; (4) a written character; (5) in various uses, representing the technical applications of the Greek *schema* (σχῆμα), for example, in "figure of speech" (*OED*, s.v. "figure"). Observing these lexicographic juxtapositions, J. Hillis Miller aptly points out that the "various meanings filtered out by the *OED* in particular examples are only a matter of emphasis in a specific usage, not a matter of exclusion. Any use of 'figure' shimmers figuratively with all its possible meanings" (2012: 57). It seems therefore useful to explore this semantic flexibility from within its open field whose meanings almost symmetrically correspond with a specific ornamental figure that comes about in the shape of decorative designs and geometric lines: the wallpaper pattern.

To reply to the former set of questions, the history of art offers a useful hint. In his *The Life of Forms in Art*, Focillon suggested that ornament not only exists "in and of itself, but it also shapes its own environment— to which it imparts a form" (1992: 66). Hardly anyone else did sum up the generative potential of the ornament's spatial production more poignantly than Focillon but the inquiry that his observation entails was left to be explored by a few artists who, quite literally, had first to nail the ornament's vertiginous motion and paste it on the wall. The question implied by Focillon's observation can be phrased as follows: If the aesthetic force of the ornament is to shape its surrounding, what happens when someone gets too close to it, will the subject also become one of its curves? That the wallpaper floral and geometric patterns stretching across the walls of interiors are a far cry from an innocent decoration but instead radically transform the human figures in their proximity while reconfiguring the surrounding space through the affective operation of saturating will be demonstrated with a cluster of both literary and scholarly writings and moving images including Nabokov's novel *Pnin* (1957), an autobiographical account by the historian Frank Ankersmit, Bergman's film *Through a Glass Darkly* (1961), Gilman's short story "The Yellow Wall-Paper" (1892), and the works of two contemporary Czech visual artists Michal Pěchouček (2004) and Jan Šerých (2005). Reading the formal metamorphoses of their ornamental patterns that trigger the affects of fascination, confusion, and fear, while often bordering with madness, and probing the ways their forms are saturated by the excess of visual or textual detail, this chapter will argue that the wallpaper disformations manifest a scene of transhistorical survival of the rococo ornamental curves and the reiteration of a radical event they brought about, one of the broken frame.

Nabokov's Unruly Geometry of Wallpaper

Right after the opening passage of the novel *Pnin* (1957), when the eponymous professor at the Waindell College finds out that he is sitting in a wrong train, Nabokov's typically ironic narrator depicts the heart attack of the main protagonist on a park bench in the small town of Cremona, indulging in a possible scenario that this odd state could well have been an effect of a "mysterious disease" or a previously eaten ham sandwich with the pickle (1989: 20). In the dazed state of his sudden seizure, Pnin faintly immerses himself into his St. Petersburg childhood, taking the reader to the hazy space of his now recovered memory. As a little eleven-year-old patient, swathed in a damp and cold cloth like "a poor cocooned pupa," half-choked by a bundle of sheets, numbed by pain, fear, and the feverish buzzing in his head, he observes the decorative design on the "four-section screen of polished wood" dividing his bed, moving on to the wall decoration, where "familiar shapes became the breeding places of evil delusions" (1989: 23). The observing narrative voice then continues:

> Still more oppressive was his tussle with the wallpaper. He had always been able to see that in the vertical plane a combination made up of three different clusters of purple flowers and seven different oak leaves was repeated a number of times with soothing exactitude; but now he was bothered by the undismissible fact that he could not find what system of inclusion and circumscription governed the horizontal recurrence of the pattern [. . .]. It stood to reason that if the evil designer—the destroyer of minds, the friend of fever— had concealed the key of the pattern with such monstrous care, that key must be as precious as life itself and, when found, would regain for Timofey Pnin his everyday health, his everyday world; and this lucid—alas, too lucid—thought forced him to persevere in the struggle. (23)

The geometric precision of this spatial recollection is striking in itself yet what gives this formalism its true tour de force is the timing for it arises at the moment when the protagonist is close to death. Just a few moments before the seizure, Pnin reaches a quasi-mystical communion with the surrounding landscape: "The sensation poor Pnin experienced was something very like that divestment, that communion. He felt porous and pregnable" (1989: 20). As if to make its fictional protagonist even more porous and ontologically dissolved—to make him, indeed, a nobody—the narrator fleetingly mentions that a human being "exists only insofar as he is separated from his surroundings" (20). Pnin's world is thus violently fragile; not only does he occur on the thin line between life and mortal agony, straddling the present moment and the scene of memory, but his both observing and deadly ill body also becomes shaped and structured by the incomprehensible, disturbing ornamental space. Through his delirious gaze captured by a complex geometry that is too rigorous to be deciphered and to yield a clear sense, he is drawn into a hallucination engendered by the wallpaper pattern.

Nabokov's predilection for wallpaper comes about not only in its repeated use across his poems and fictions but also in his pedagogical practice.[1] His famous biographer Brian Boyd drew up the following anecdote related to the author's appointment at Cornell University in 1958 and his unusual way of teaching literary history with the proverbial emphasis on details:

> When the exam came on March 19, he asked the students a question they would never forget, even if they could not recall the answer: "Describe the wallpaper in the Karenins' bedroom." Answer: part 4, chapter 17: Anna, expected to die of puerperal fever [. . .] points at the wallpaper and exclaims, "How tastelessly these flowers are done, not at all like violets."[2] (1991: 358)

Without any of such aesthetic judgment yet with all the stronger geometric fascination in *Pnin*, the hermeneutics of wallpaper—that is searching for a clue to the wallpaper pattern and a desire to discover the system in order to enter the imaginary world—is underlaid not only by a hope of recovery and a rational distance of the observing subject from the hallucination-provoking object but also by the possibility of a shift from the real to the phantasmatic world: "And although the witness and victim of these phantasms was tucked up in bed, he was, in accordance with the twofold nature of his surroundings, simultaneously seated on a bench in a green and purple park" (24). Since any phantasm is always the "imaginary scenario" that figures a fulfilling of the conscious or unconscious desire (Laplanche and Pontalis 2009: 152), the text follows the script in echoing the precise, purple and green, colors of the wallpaper.[3] While the wallpaper pattern first stands for a therapeutic riddle, which, if solved, could rid little Pnin of his illness, it gradually assumes the form of a hallucinatory medium, enabling an imaginary as well as physical shift across space and time, between two completely different worlds of then and now.

However, since in Nabokov's world one conundrum is always but an opening toward another one—the same way Kafka's potentially infinite gates in the *Trial* (1925) lead only to another bigger gates, guarded by another and more powerful gatekeepers—the polymorphous world and identity of the protagonist is but a narrative hors d'oeuvre inviting to the true finesse of the narrator's games. As the voice belonging to the delirious Pnin tells us, the wallpaper is a product of "the evil designer" ("the destroyer of minds, the friend of fever") who happens to be, in turn, created by the protagonist's feverish mind. At the same time, however, the evil designer is a demiurge of the whole depicted world, a textual architect of the diegetic space. In the preceding dense passage the textual medium mirrors itself offering a vertiginous—because a two-way—mise en abyme: both the delirious child and the adult Pnin are simultaneously found on the park bench, while the narrator lurks from behind the wallpaper pattern—with a mirror in his hand, gleefully indulging in his metaleptic maneuvers.

Inasmuch as the purple flowers and oak leaves of the wall decoration provide the longed-for hermeneutic key for the protagonist, the same illusion ensnares the readers who weave their way through the text just as little Pnin does through the wallpaper pattern. The texture of the enigmatic wallpaper, mischievously hiding and revealing its diegetic composer, is analogous to the tissue of the whole text wherein the designer is exposed by no one else than Pnin himself toward the end of the novel.[4] His embittered outcry against the narrator going by name of Vladimir Vladimirovich during a communal dinner makes this analogy even more obvious: "Now, don't believe a word he says, Georgiy Aramovich. He makes up everything [. . .]. He is a dreadful inventor [on uzhasniy vidumshchik]" (185). In a wink to the Pirandellian rebellion of theater characters against their author, the former "evil designer"— that is the choreographer of the unruly geometry who draws both Pnins (the eleven-year-old and the adult one) into the hallucinatory logic of the wallpaper patterns—becomes a "dreadful inventor" in the adult Pnin's outburst against his position of a mere narrative invention.

Rococo, or the Broken Frame

But what are those floral designs on the wallpaper both observed and
steered by the delirious child's gaze and, at the same time, by the adult
Pnin during his heart attack—and what is their formal and affective
agency? It is neither a mere realist representation of plants and trees nor
a purely accidental assemblage of lines and shapes, but the *ornamental
pattern*: a nonmimetic abstraction and geometric composition—an
ornament that does not represent natural forms and floral vegetation but
rather suggests and evokes their vivacity. To understand these geometric
lines animated with organic rhythms that "evoke growth and movement
without falling into representation" (Grabar 1992: 224), we need to
delve into one of its key moments, the rococo era, which is commonly
associated with its supposedly shallow and superficial decorative
attributes, though a fleeting glance at a few artworks of this intermedia
style will show the powerful potential it has for the contemporary media
reflection. Since the original homeland of the rococo style, commonly
dated between 1690 and 1750, is the field of decorative art cultivated
throughout private spaces of the Parisian parlors, it has been overlooked
for a long time as a mere transitional phase between the monumental
baroque and the ancient symmetry-seeking neoclassicism but also as a
fad of an excessive ornamentation, a useless and distractive flamboyance,
and a manifestation of a visual pomp, frivolity, and even libertinism
(Berchtold, Démoris, and Martin 2012: 8).[5]

   In the first half of the eighteenth century in France, a remarkable
aesthetic event took place thanks to several visual artists and architects
serving at the court of Louis XV whose engravings and drawings find
a common ground in the themes and techniques of ornamentation
rendered on the decorative cartouche designs. Although in part already
present in the late baroque arabesques of such artists as Jean Bérain the
Elder, Pierre Lepautre, and Jean-Antoin Watteau, art historians situate
the birth of the specific ornamental mode as a pure invention of the
rococo era around 1830.[6] The engravings of Juste-Aurèle Meissonnier,
Jacques de Lajoue, and François de Cuvilliés introduced a new form of
ornament called *rocaille*, one that was composed of diverse modifications
of the shell motif along with the richly intertwined C-shaped curves and
lines. In these rocaille formations, as Karsten Harries observes, the shell
is "transformed into an almost abstract, endlessly malleable material,
out of which the artist molds landscapes and fantastic architectures"
(1983: 10). Hence the *rocaille* form is born as soon as "the shell motif,

Figure 2.1 Jacques de Lajoue, *Second livre de tableaux et rocailles*, 1734. Museum für angewandte Kunst (MAK), Wien. Wikimedia Commons.

a common element of the edges and frames of grotesques, becomes the center of the composition" (1983: 10).[7] Refusing to remain limited by its carrier—the frame—the rococo ornament leaves the edges of the picture and invades its center to become an autonomous aesthetic object (Figure 2.1).

Such a spatial inversion has clearly quite radical consequences for the decorative status of the ornament which, as Winfried Menninghaus notes, acquires a hybrid ontological condition grounded in an inter-position between the pictorial and the ornamental mode:

> In the rocaille ornament, shell work and leaf work is extended from the frame onto what is enframed until it largely comes to substitute for the image itself. From this a hybrid emerges that is neither simply image nor ornament. In becoming an image-object whose representation provides the impression of a spatial depth, the ornament gradually emancipates itself from the flatness of the surface to which it is applied [. . .]. Oscillating between the modes of ornament and imagery, the new treatment of ornamental framing brings forth a "world of its own" that consists of ideal (quasi-) objects. (1999: 73)

During the rococo period, ornament hence ceases to stand for a mere decoration, an embellishment independent of the overall structure, turning instead into a dominant visual medium. At first glance, there is nothing dramatic about Lajoue's engraving but under closer scrutiny, within the spectacular renderings of stone stairways, fountains, or human figures that adopt the undulating and coquettishly swinging movement of the surrounding architecture, something more takes place. Something that defies the notion of ornament which has prevailed in Western aesthetic discourse until today and whose founding definition was introduced by Kant in his *Critique of the Power of Judgment* (1790) via the term *parergon* that signifies not only a non-functional embellishment but also a decorative supplement which does not participate in the inner structure of artwork:

> Even what one calls ornaments (*parerga*), i.e., that which is not internal to the entire representation of the object as a constituent, but only belongs to it externally as an addendum and augments the satisfaction of taste, still does this only through its form: like the borders of paintings, draperies on statues, or colonnades around magnificent buildings. But if the ornament itself does not consist in beautiful form, if it is, like a gilt frame, attached merely in order to recommend approval for the painting through its charm— then it is called decoration, and detracts from genuine beauty. (2000: 110–11)

Yet the aesthetic quasi-objects and hybrid media do not always follow Kantian prescriptions and although this definition is uncritically rehearsed by scholars until today, the affective and formal work of ornament this chapter explores could not be further from its traditional externalizing view.[8] More than a half a century before the publication of Kant's treatise, the abundantly illustrated book *Livre d'ornemens* (The Book of Ornaments, 1734) designed by Meissonnier was published, one that displayed the playful ornamental curves meandering in the dynamic form of waves and shells. Interconnecting two-dimensional linearity of the decorative frame with the depths of the inner pictorial world, these ornamental curves represent nothing but themselves and are nothing less than a vigorous deconstruction of Kant's notion of the extrinsic addition (Figure 2.2).[9]

While strictly opposed to the Kantian *parergon*, the visual movement and aesthetic performativity of the rococo ornamental curves find their conceptual correlate in the way Derrida elaborates the same term in

Abb. 45. Juste-Aurèle Meissonnier, Stich aus dem Livre d'ornemens, 1734

Figure 2.2 Juste-Aurèle Meissonnier, *Livre d'ornemens*, 1734. Rijksmuseum, Amsterdam. Wikimedia Commons.

his *The Truth in Painting* (1978). Drawing on the etymological roots of the concept, based on a compound of the Greek *ergon* (work) and *para* (above, beyond, beside), Derrida explains *parergon* as something strongly *atopic*—not an artwork itself and even less existing beyond it: "neither inside nor outside, neither above nor below, it disconcerts any opposition but does not remain indeterminate and it *gives rise* to the work" (1987: 9). Like the rococo ornament, whose lines move freely between the frame and the center of the image, the Derridean *parergon* too dissolves the alleged boundaries between interior and exterior, disrupting the hierarchic opposition of the visual center and the decorative periphery, ultimately challenging the very notions of the "central" dominant and the "added" element. As elegantly noticed by Menninghaus, "parerga are para-sitic in a double sense: first, they are spatially situated next to an ergon; second, they draw from it their power and the particular surplus of their being" (1999: 81). Furthermore, *parergon* complicates that Kantian dichotomy between the core *ergon* and its additional element not only within a given image but also in itself:

What constitutes them as *parerga* is not simply their exteriority as a surplus, it is the internal structural link which rivets them to the lack in the interior of the *ergon*. And this lack would be constitutive of

the very unity of the *ergon*. Without this lack, the *ergon* would have
no need of a *parergon*. The *ergon*'s lack is the lack of a *parergon*, of
the garment or the column which nevertheless remains exterior to
it. (Derrida 1987: 59)

To see how to situate this paradoxical and "para-sitic" in-betweenness
of ornament, we need to pause a bit more with rococo and its undoing
of representation. As Frank Ankersmit emphasizes in his take on
rocaille that will be discussed in more detail further, the hierarchical
relationship between reality and ornament is overturned, for the real
world with its nature, architecture, and human beings is no longer a
source of mimesis: "Rococo ornament invades reality by ornament:
the objects of representation adapt themselves to ornament" (2003:
150). But how to explain such an emancipation and, consequently,
formal saturation of what were once but playful undulating lines, firmly
tied to their framework? The answer that rococo scholars suggest is
unequivocal: the frame, that had by then kept the distance between
the actual and the fictional world, has broken. Taking his cue from this
overturned representation and disrupted framing, Harries therefore
argues for rococo as a "threshold that both separates and links" the old
art, faithful to representation, and modern art that "gestures towards art
for art's sake" (1989: 80–2).[10]

    In his close reading of the copper plate entitled *Der liebe Morgen*
(The Dear Morning, *c.* 1770) by the German engraver Johann Esaias
Nilson, Harries demonstrates how the functional frame, whose goal
was originally to separate the pictorial representation from the real
world and thus enhance the former's autonomy, becomes *self-referential*,
drawing attention to itself while engendering a playful deconstruction
of the depicted world. Both the pastoral and love theme of this placid
and seemingly idyllic scene is quickly superseded by a confusing mise-
en-scène whereby the center of the image is occupied by nothing but
an odd and somewhat impossible frame (Figure 2.3). At first glance,
this frame is supposed to encircle the female figure leaning out of the
window and exchanging the glance with the lover, who blows the horn
just below, yet this conventional logic is subverted by the fact that
the octagonal frame is a ruin that, moreover, rises from a crumbling
pedestal. Looking back at the rococo engravings, this broken frame, at
once framing and unframing, ornamental and pictorial, blurring the
difference between inside and outside, can thus help to understand the
breaking of the frame as a generative event of disformation, whose main
actors are the subversive proliferating ornamental curves and whose

Figure 2.3 Johann Esaias Nilson, *Der liebe Morgen, c.* 1770. Museum für angewandte Kunst (MAK), Wien. Wikimedia Commons.

formal disturbances move both inward and outward, forcing to adapt everything they encounter to their strange forms.

While Ankersmit provides the case of the inner pictorial deformation when observing that the rococo "ornamental forms have penetrated into the picture center [. . .] and have become *themselves* potential objects of depiction" (2003: 144), Harries helps to understand the outward movement that is possible only due to the broken rococo frame. By no means does the performative force of these unruly lines end at this particular historical moment; quite the contrary: due to the crack in the frame, the ornamental curves have grown out of their broken framework to assume new media forms and sustain their aesthetic logic in other places and at other times. As I will argue further, one of the sites of the rococo survival are the ornamental wallpaper patterns that repeat the same performative motion, forcing their geometric structure upon their surroundings while absorbing the human figures in their proximity to finally make them a part of their composition.

Boredom, Fascination, and the Screen of Hallucination

Let us now return to the relationship between the ornamental pattern of wallpaper and the observing subject. While Nabokov's novel theorizes this link by means of the complex diegetic shifting enabled by the geometric logic of the confusing patterns, the link also reveals a generative affective agency that was so far put aside and that plays a crucial role in Ankersmit's take on rococo ornament. As suggested by the title of his essay "Rococo as the Dissipation of Boredom," the author draws on a biographical experience of ennui during the frequent illnesses in his childhood. In a state that smacks of the feverish gaze of Nabokov's little Pnin—but equally reminiscent of the famous opening passage from Proust's *Swann's Way* (1913), wherein the narrator immerses into a child memory of longing for his mother's coming to his bedroom in Combray—he was forced to stay in bed for lengthy days, tangled in the bedsheets and idly watching his surroundings:

> Overwhelmed by boredom, I often felt a peculiar fascination for the flower patterns on the curtains in my parents' bedroom. And I am convinced of an intimate connection between those feelings of boredom on the one hand and fascination, on the other. The intimacy of this connection is at first sight paradoxical, since boredom seems to exclude us from reality and all that goes on in it, whereas fascination (derived from the Latin *fasces*, meaning a bundle or truss) clearly suggests the tying together of subject and object. (2003: 132)

While Ankersmit spells out boredom as a temporary suspension of the interactions between ourselves and the world, one that "invites reality to manifest its true nature untainted and undistorted by our interests and preoccupations," and explains fascination as a tantalizing and unfulfilled promise of a fusion between the subject and object (132), what makes the ornamental patterns come alive and activate their formal affordances is the very combination and interactivity of both of these affects. Moreover, if, as Ankersmit advises, we manage to refrain from viewing the particular design as a mimetic representation of, say, a real flower and recognize it instead as a non-referential pattern, we will see how the shapes on the wallpaper begin to intertwine and assume new formations in motion.

Before delving into the intricacies of cultural history of the rococo ornament, Ankersmit attempts to account for his fascination with the flower patterns through Roger Scruton's useful analogy between the nonrepresentational stone leaf-moldings in Gothic architecture and the stylized flowers in a dress or a piece of wallpaper: "There is all the difference in the world between the pattern of wallpaper and a picture of the thing used in the pattern: even if they look exactly the same. The wallpaper is not asking us to think of the flowers contained in it" (Scruton 1997: 121; qtd. in Ankersmit 2003: 133). Even though Ankersmit pays a meticulous attention to the ornamental framework in the rococo engravings, what remains overshadowed by his fascination with the anatomy and movement of the ornamental curves is the fact that the ornamental pattern—be it imprinted into a wallpaper or a curtain—*lacks* a fixed frame. Yet it is precisely this *parergonal* lack of the frame what allows the floral designs to easily leave the space of the wall and invade the surrounding space, blending with the present objects and subjects. What is more, due to the very absence of a frame the wallpaper pattern absorbs the beholder into its morphology and entangles them within the confusing lines of its ornamental core. As a result of both the fissure of the rococo frame and the absorbing nonmimetic wallpaper pattern, the excessive movement of the ornamental curves triggers an affective operation of saturating that structures the observing subject's mind and gaze.

The formal affinity between the generative movement of the rococo ornament and the saturating wallpaper patterns has also its historical grounding for, as art historians demonstrate, this interior decoration came to fashion at the same moment the ornamental *rocaille* style was at the height if its fame.[11] Along with the usual floral and abstract motifs of the wallpaper geometric arabesques, some of the English wallpapers from the mid-eighteenth century reveal sophisticated compositions with an ornamentalized self-referential frame. An observation Jean Starobinski made about the rococo aesthetics that "loves to ironize its own fictions" (1987: 39) thus holds equally true for the meta-illusionary wallpaper designs that use its historically broken frame in a two-way direction: to invade the surrounding space and to absorb the subjects therein. However, while in the history of design and architecture, the protean wallpaper adapted to all current styles and artistic needs and thus dominantly served as "a means of expressing individual personality in private spaces" (Thibaut-Pomerantz 2009: 235), the modern and contemporary aesthetic forms replace this adaptability with the desubjectifying operationality sustained by a media inversion. The point of this inversion lies in that the wallpaper is no longer a means of expressing or otherwise representing the subject, but quite the contrary: *the subject follows the ornamental form.*

The formal saturation that Nabokov plays out via both the diegetic and discursive geometry of the wallpaper and that Ankersmit describes by means of the immersive movement of the ornamental curves is compellingly taken up by Bergman in his film *Through a Glass Darkly* (1961) wherein the wallpapers provide not only a phantasmatic screen but also an audiovisual space of the subject's absorption. In what is perhaps the most enigmatic scene of the film, structured as a three-act stage play about a drama of one family (Karin, her father David, brother Minus, and husband Martin) vacationing on a remote island retreat, the main protagonist Karin, who suffers from schizophrenia and related auditory hallucinations, sets out for an abandoned attic room in the dim light of dawn, accompanied by the blowing of a distant lighthouse foghorn. At the moment when she appears in front of the faded and torn wallpaper in a tight close-up, touching it gently with her palms, the camera reveals the flame-like shimmers of the rising sun on the leafy wallpaper designs, to finally track in to another close-up of a black slit emitting insisting but incomprehensible female and male whispers to which Karin attentively listens in her white nightgown (Figure 2.4).

Figure 2.4 A screen capture from Ingmar Bergman, *Through a Glass Darkly* (1961). Criterion Collection, 2003. DVD.

Stepping back softly after a countershot through the window on the rising sun and against the sonic backdrop of the continual murmur of voices, she folds her hands with her lips, silently repeating the inarticulate voices coming from the wall and sighing. After a short moment of caressing her hips and hair, she starts violently rubbing her thighs, whereupon her body contorts in a cramp and she falls to her knees in a convulsive movement of masturbation. As her hands suddenly hit the floor and her body collapses to the ground, the ornamental mode of her convoluted gestures is interrupted, the voices die away, and her eyes and facial expression take on a conscious yet exhausted look.

According to Alexis Luko, both diegetic sounds that frame and punctuate the dramatic scenes, the D-F tones of foghorn and the roar of helicopter (that takes Karin away from the island to the hospital) intermingle with the main—and non-diegetic—musical motif of Bach's Sarabande from *Cello Suite No. 2* in D minor. In contrast with his suggestion that Karin "revel[s] in aural communion with a sound that transports her to a state of ecstasy" (2016: 126), I want to propose a spatial reading of this scene that uncovers the parallel between her contortion and the ornamental curves driving both the visual movement of the wallpaper design and her schizophrenic vision. That the hallucinatory voices are heard behind the torn wallpaper pattern is hardly accidental; by means of its proliferating movement with which it inscribes the rhythmical patterns into the wall, the ornament reinforces the hallucinatory vision and drives the movement of the protagonist's body.[12] As we learn later, at the start of Act II, from Karin's conversation with her brother Minus in the same attic room and just a moment before their off-screen incestuous union, these expeditions to the voice behind the wallpaper take place regularly at dawn. With a mysterious smile, Karin goes on to depict: "One day someone called to me from behind the wallpaper [. . .]. The voice went on calling me, so I pressed myself against the wall and it opened up like a lot of leaves *and there I was inside*" (Bergman 1970: 42). She then tells the terrified Minus about a light, spacious, and quiet room full of human figures walking around with their faces bright in the anticipation of seeing God. Yet the god who comes to Karin in the final dramatic scene through the half-opened wallpapered closet door in the attic room is not the longed-for god of love but a stony-faced spider god who tries to rape her. Rather than making analogies between this fearful hallucination of a rapist arachnid and Karin's family members who, each in their own term, do take advantage of her, I want to argue that precisely as in Nabokov's *Pnin*, the dreadful force behind the wallpaper *is not metaphorical but morphological*: the subject has no other choice than to follow the ornamental form.

   Unsurprisingly, Torsten Jungstedt explains Karin's entrance into the haunted world through the wallpapers as a reference to the famous American short story "The Yellow Wall-Paper" (1892) written by Charlotte Perkins Gilman that he allegedly gave Bergman to read and the filmmaker, in turn, used it as the basis for his finally unrealized color film *Wallpaper*, the original version of *Through a Glass Darkly* (Gado 2007: 272). Whether or not one relies this on biographical account, it is now time to take a closer look at the possible pretext of Bergman's wallpaper inspiration. Not in order to track down a potential source of influence but rather to show that on its way from rococo engravings to the late modern and contemporary wallpapers, the ornamental curves made an interlude at the end of the nineteenth century to break not only a visual frame but also the discursive one.

For a Morphological Reading of Gilman's Wallpaper

We might perhaps never have been modern but our wallpapers certainly have. The so far described features of the wallpaper surface— the phantasmatic space that shapes an observing subject while providing a false hermeneutic key, the dynamic rocaille survivals, the invasion into the lived space of interiors—have their striking modernist manifestation in the short story "The Yellow Wall-Paper" by Charlotte Perkins Gilman (1892). Not only do the wallpaper metamorphoses stand for a focal point around which the whole narrative revolves but, more importantly, the proliferating ornamental patterns also ceaselessly generate disformations whose affective agency and formal motion penetrate the protagonist's discourse to finally shape and structure the entire text. As a result, the narrative dispenses with the realistic qualities on the way to releasing an ornamental excess mediated by the rhythmical metamorphoses which blur temporal and spatial levels and trigger an illogical and even contradictory movement of language. Even though a staggering amount of scholarship has accumulated around this famous piece of Gilman's writing since its reissue by The Feminist Press in 1973, the following section will take a look at what remains almost entirely overlooked: a speculative potential with which the text counters its dominant allegorical readings en route to manifest a theoretical force of ornamental forms and their media operationality. While most scholars read the story as an biographical "feminist manifesto" (Doran 2013: 73) of the gender emancipation from the oppressive masculine forces and "patriarchal oppression" (St. Jean 2002: 412), I will argue that such an allegorical reading is a methodological trap that can best be avoided by following the formal moves of the text that shifts from the allegorical and hence representational regime to its affective performativity.[13]

Without a doubt, both the personal biography and storyline give every good reason to understand Gilman's piece as the allegory of an emancipation from the woman imprisonment and a fictionalized account of her nervous breakdown in 1887. An anonymous young female protagonist suffering from anxiety—with the evident signs of a postpartum psychosis—becomes in part voluntarily, in part by an order of her husband and physician, John, a prisoner in her wallpapered room, progressively descending into madness, becoming obsessed by the specters that are looming behind the soiled yellow wallpaper, its patterns and stains. The entanglement of John's keeping her under lock, the indications of a sinister past and violence that took place in her gloomy room, and the detailed descriptions of the wallpaper patterns and designs that continually reveal dramatic scenery wherein a mysterious female figure takes shape, looming behind the patterns as if behind the iron bars and attempting to get away— all this, indeed, suggests a symbolical meaning of imprisonment and desire for liberation. Such a reading is only reinforced by the very behavior of the main protagonist throughout the narrative, who, at first, tries to help rescue the female figures with whom she identifies only to finally transform into one of them. Yet before one eagerly falls into certitudes of a symptomatic reading that unearths the prisonlike bars of the wallpaper design as a "metaphoric space" for the shifting masculine and feminine selves (Rogers 1998: 52), or diagnoses the protagonist's deciphering of the ornamental patterns as a "a case of hysterical (over)reading" (Jacobus 2014: 96)—a classifying reading, in short, that usually begins far *before* and *outside* the text—it is important to take a closer look at both the anatomy and physiology of the living wallpaper patterns while paying attention to the ways their visual motion penetrates the movement of discourse.

First of all, the tone of the wallpaper's description is highly ambiguous and while the material layer is itself "repellant, almost revolting," "faded" and "smouldering unclean yellow" that emanates a peculiar "yellow smell" (2009: 168, 178), even more troubling is the pattern that the protagonist observes day and night with a mix of fascination and irritation:

> It is dull enough to confuse the eye in following, pronounced enough to constantly irritate and provoke study, and when you follow the

lame uncertain curves for a little distance they suddenly commit suicide—plunge off at outrageous angles, destroy themselves in unheard of contradictions. (168)

Combining the monotonous repetitive pattern with a sort of hypnotic charm and a powerful synesthesia blending the "haptic opticality" (Doran 2013: 75) with the visual and sonic effects, the moving wallpaper anatomy generates a formation that immerses both the protagonist's and reader's gaze into its affective and sensory dynamics. The recursive pattern produces a space of animating curves that by far exceed a traditional personification on the way to playing out a scene of a hybrid structural morphing, which has only little (if anything at all) to do with the original purpose of decoration. One the one hand, the wallpaper subverts any decorative utility via its evocation of "a kind of 'debased Romanesque' with *delirium tremens*" (172), on the other, the last remnants of a decorative function are dissolved due to the floral proliferation whereby "the sprawling outlines run off in great slanting waves of optic horror, like a lot of wallowing seaweeds in full chase" (172). Rather than a "'patriarchal text' in which literary women—in fact, all women—are trapped" (Hochman 2002: 91), this breakneck organic motion of the artificial ornamental curves echo Giovanni Battista Piranesi's rococo sceneries staging nocturnal Roman ruins swallowed and pervaded by a proliferating vegetation. It would be certainly tempting to parse the analogy between, on the one hand, what rococo scholars call the "language of incongruity" grounded in distortions, deformations, and inaccuracies of the decorative vocabulary and aesthetic syntax (Michel 1984: 131) and, on the other, Gilman's phantasmagorical wallpaper morphology—that the protagonist compares to a rhizomatic organism whose biological taxonomy lies on a scale between plants and animals, namely fungus growing on the walls as "an interminable string of toadstools, budding and sprouting in endless convolution" (175)—which pervades the protagonist's mind. But since representation is the least interesting quality of ornament in its both rococo and modernist extensions, perpetually seducing to a symbolical reading at that, we should now turn to what this ornamental figure actually *does* with and to its discursive space.

Induced by its confusing linear designs, the wallpaper catalyzes an important shift in identities, preceded by a mutual blending of the protagonist's and the pattern's gazes. For the obsessive effort to decipher the ornamental pattern and distinguish the shapes emerging against its background is but one aspect of interaction between the observing subject and the observed surface, an interaction that ultimately puts in question such distinctions and culminates into their inversion during which the observed object becomes the very beholder. "This paper looks to me as if it *knew* what a vicious influence it had! There is a recurrent spot where the pattern lolls like a broken neck and two bulbous eyes stare at you upside down" (170). Yet there is more to this scopic frenzy of the returning uncanny gaze because those omnipresent "absurd, unblinking eyes" (170) that stare at the protagonist from behind the patterns do not belong to anyone else than to herself. Precisely in the manner of the puzzling ornamental motion, this shift in gazes opens up another swap, the one of identities. Throughout the narrative, the affinity between the mysterious female figures imprisoned inside the pattern and the protagonist remains implicit but toward the end, the text leaves no doubt that the scrutinized creeping wallpaper figure is but the protagonist herself: "I suppose I shall have to get back behind the pattern when it comes night, and that is hard!" (181). As a result of this simple switch of pronouns, we are left with a weird denouement as it is no more clear whether the protagonist tries to set the wallpaper figures free or, on the contrary, to tie them up with a rope at hand.

It is precisely at this moment that the so far logically composed diegesis is swirled into a subversive whirl of the ornament that extends from the space of the wall to penetrate the very medium that gives it its shape, meaning, and affective force: the medium of language. Hardly by accident, the repetitive pirouettes of the ornamental curves enter the discursive structure when the protagonist struggles to comprehend the dynamic transformations of the wallpaper pattern: "I wonder how it was done and who did it, and what they did it for. Round and round and round—round and round and round—it makes me dizzy!" (178). In order for the pattern to reproduce its main morphological principle, that is recursivity in terms of a self-generating and autoreferential repetition, the insistent lexicon— revolving around the syllabic flood of nearly dozen "o"s, which rigorously iterate both the round form of the goggling eyes and the stupefied open mouth and which are literally crammed between the edges made of the subject's pronouns—drives and gives rhythm to the circular syntax.

And this is also where the formal affects of curiosity, dizziness, and confusion make up the operative movement of *saturation* whose Latin etymological root *satis*—enough—implies a twofold meaning. First, that the ornamental form here is charged with those prolific patterns to the point where nothing more can be absorbed or retained; second, the formal excess of visual details voices its only possible response: *satis!* The saturation of form that disturbs and subsequently reconfigures the subject according to the logic of disformation thus not only invokes the affective force "that does not have to move from subject to object but may fold back, rebound, recursively amplify" (Brinkema 2014: 24) but also performs such a recursive movement in the direction from the wallpaper object to the subject of protagonist.

Far from occurring isolated in the narrator's silent monologue, the incongruous logic of ornament also enters her repetitive direct speech when the story nears its dramatic climax during which she locks herself in the room, throws the key out of the window and sets up to a frenzy tearing down and biting off the wallpaper. While just a moment before she steadily announces to the reader having "locked the door and thrown the key down into the front path" (181), right after that, a sneaking irony tinges her voice when stating with a slightly different tone: "'John dear!'" said I in the gentlest voice, 'the key is down by the front steps, under a plantain leaf!'" (182), to round it up with a subtle modification: "'The key is down by the front door under a plantain leaf!'" (182). In addition, she keeps repeating her line several times yet "very gently and slowly" until John actually finds the key (182). For all the temptation to read this exalted moment of the wallpaper's destruction allegorically—as an unabashed stripping away of the normative phallogocentrist layers aimed at a recovery of the true feminine self and realized through a bodily revolt and a few verbal tricks—following the performative logic of ornament which, once again, drives the narrative, structures the text, and saturates both the visual and discursive forms, it seems more appropriate to linger on the structural element that moves both the diegetic space and the protagonist's language. This structure is built upon a repetitive pattern yet does not come about as a well-known Deleuzian repetition with difference but rather as a *repetition with contradiction*.[14]

In other words, from the point of view of the textual performativity it is not a metaphorical—and thus predetermined—meaning that comes to the fore but rather the fact that the literary language takes up and reproduces the convoluted movement of the ornamental pattern. The best evidence for such a morphological reading is provided by the protagonist's performance insofar as her own body reproduces and morphs into the ornamental curves moving along the room: "But here I can creep smoothly on the floor, and my shoulder just fits in that long smooch around the wall, so I cannot lose my way" (182). Consequently, the creeping ornamental dance opens up the dramatic finale:

"What is the matter?" he cried. "For God's sake, what are you doing!"
I kept on creeping just the same, but I looked at him over my shoulder.

"I've got out at last," said I, "in spite of you and Jane! And I've pulled off most of the paper, so you can't put me back!"
Now why should that man have fainted? But he did, and right across my path by the wall, so that I had to creep over him every time! (182)

As if to endorse both the narrative's enactment of that ornamental contradictory movement and counter-allegorical reading of the text, the allegedly oppressive figure of John suddenly becomes a mere depersonalized "that man" who matters to the protagonist—and thus to the whole text structured by the ornamental mode of *her* language— only inasmuch as he or, rather, *it* is an annoying and purely material obstacle that needs to be crawled over in the rhythm of the wallpaper pattern. The same ornamental excess that once resulted in the crack in the frame on the rococo engravings, blending the world inside and outside the picture and imprinting its contours on the outer reality now breaks through the symbolic and discursive frame in Gilman's text. While at the allegorical level the constricting gender, power, and psychological confines are burst open under the pressure of the wallpaper "*pattern*alistic" narrative, the affective and formal force of the ornamental disformations undo the media boundaries between the discursive and the visual, the image and the text. Because the visual ornament has invaded the language which then continues to reproduce its forms, paradoxical logic, and excessive movement, "The Yellow Wall-Paper" shows that the media excess cannot be thought without the affective dynamic triggered by movement of forms.

Between Excess and Absence: The Patterns of Madness

In place of conclusion, I want to offer an overview of two much less known and yet highly relevant works that extend the rococo generative deformations to the contemporary art and thus enhance the opening suggestion about the transhistorical motion of the ornamental figure and its survival within the wallpaper patterns. The phantasm of the merging of the subject and object along with the mutual shaping of the human physiognomy and its surrounding space take place on both the visual and sonic level in a 2004 video by the contemporary multimedia artist Michal Pěchouček. Its title *Pram Room* (*Kočárkárna*) alludes to the typical architectural vocabulary of the socialist era, with its fancy for large prefab housing estates that Pěchouček unambiguously refers to as "the 1980s ugly design" of normalization (Mazanec 2007: 86). By means of the juxtaposed photographs of unspecified gloomy spaces, the image moves vertically in an escalating rhythm, underlaid by rumbling industrial noises and gradual howls, descending to an underground landscape, only to uncover the high-rise flat of the protagonist and his or her wallpapered bedroom where a peculiar explosion of decorative patterns takes place. While the protagonist dressed in the flowered housecoat is continually revealed to be performed in a queer fashion by the artist himself, the overall narrative indicates the suicide of a lonely woman—a certain Marie M. (as the DVD sheet explains)—presented through the sequence of ghostly tableaux.

Once inside the underground bedroom, the viewers are presented with a bizarre indoor greenhouse, although it is not living plants that reigns here but the flower patterns spread all over the walls, the protagonist's housecoat, and the blanket on a bed. The only spot that remains not covered by the patterns is the face of the protagonist whose wide-eyed expression on one of the moving photographs underscores the uncanny framing of the whole scene (Figure 2.5).

Figure 2.5 Still from Michal Pěchouček, *Pram Room* (2004). *Pater Noster Video Stories*. Jiri Svestka Gallery, 2009. DVD. Courtesy of the artist.

Paradoxical as it may sound, given the overwhelming floral opulence, the video "hybrid moving images" suggest neither a dynamic vegetal growth nor an abundant fertility but quite the contrary: the motion seems to be frozen and its stiff choreography not only prefigures the later suicide but also self-reflectively mirrors its own photographic mediation.[15] Rather than relying on a predictable camp aesthetics, the ornamental excess—fully coextensive with the ominous rumbling sounds—structures the claustrophobic mise-en-scène, saturating the enclosed space with an atmosphere of solitude. To materialize, as it were, the seemingly light-hearted metaphor of "pushing up the daisies," the human figure turns into a living corpse and becomes both the subject and the object of a *lifeless* still life. And this is where the morbid flower patterns take up the frame-breaking movement of the ornament as they extend from the surface to enter the diegetic space, announcing the protagonist's death.

To live up to the aesthetic and conceptual qualities of ornament, however, one should not dismiss its artistic afterlives, in this case a reframing that this photographic tableau underwent in 2008 when published on the cover of the Czech *Labyrint revue* annual magazine's special issue on the self-portraiture. For as soon as the photograph is taken out of the video and its sonic grounding, both the affective and formal work of ornamental excess described before appear in a rather comic light and without those macabre ramifications. Once the tableau is isolated, the floral patterns reveal the saturation of forms within the wallpapered seclusion of the protagonist, turning the interior of the bedroom into a phantasmagorical den of the eccentric dandy whose fancy for decoration got somewhat out of control. Despite this self-ironic gesture—that perfectly corresponds to the ceaselessly self-subverting logic of the ornamental pattern—Pěchouček's theatrical staging, the ornamental background, and the protagonist's pose altogether open up a wide range of more or less implicit visual intertexts that only reinforce the transhistorical framework and motion of ornament.

Exposing the body that disappears under the weight of the ornamental metamorphosis on the flowered housecoat, over the garish blanket, and among the leafy wallpaper patterns, this tableau echoes what Deleuze playfully dubbed "le pli all-over" (1988: 166), that is, the neo-baroque tendency of modern art to excessively cover the entire surface of the canvas with folds over folds and thus "up to infinity" (2006: 140).[16] While a certain awkwardness of the floral composition combining aggressive, at places splashy, colors and faded hues seems as if a bricoleur in the normalization era of the mid-1980s tried to reenact one of August Klimt's paintings from his "golden era" in front of a mirror, the tableau pays a more explicit charming tribute to Balthus' masterful combination of eroticism and narcissistic gestures surrounded by the hypnotic geometric patterns of the textile surfaces and wallpapers as rendered in his painting *La chambre turque* (The Turkish Room, 1963–66; Figure 2.6).

Finally, the ornamental blending of body with the decorative background and patterned surfaces is also reminiscent of several symbolist canvases by Édouard Vuillard such as *La lectrice* (The Reader, 1896)—where the intimate and contemplative atmosphere is emphasized by the fact that the volume of individual figures is literally absorbed by the thickly layered wallpaper patterns and the fabric on the richly decorated sofa—and *La coiffeuse* (The Dressing Table, 1895). On this painting, the face of one of the figures is blurred by an abundant flower bouquet and the outburst of strongly contrasting colors covering the wallpapered wall, from which shimmers of light and autumn leaves seem to fall down directly onto the ginger hair and dress of a girl turning her back on the viewer. Underlying this latent intertextual dialogue and media hybridity, Pěchouček's tableau is an exemplary

Figure 2.6 Balthus, *La chambre turque*, 1963–1966. Musée Nationale d'Art Moderne, Paris. Wikimedia Commons.

manifestation not only of the transhistorical motion of ornament but also of the affective force with which it absorbs the subjects into the wallpaper's geometric patterns.

If the affective operation of saturating released and driven by the patterns of wallpaper reconfigures the surrounding space according to the logic ornament, the subject not only is entangled into its formal dynamic but also becomes structured by it—to such an extent that a traditional notion of the self-contained autonomous subject makes no more sense. Such an avenue of desubjectification is pursued by Jan Šerých in his 2005 large-format wall painting whose very title *Kubrick's Carpet* leaves no doubt as to the intermedia strategy with which ornament proliferates via its own iterations and spatial shifts. What looks at first glance as an enlarged macro-picture of an insect eye, is a hand painting of the computer graphic rendering of the carpet design that covers the infamous second floor of the Overlook Hotel in Stanley Kubrick's film *The Shining* (1980). It is crucial to experience Šerých's painting in situ in order to fully appreciate its main compositional twofold "trick" consisting in that the classical two-dimensionality of the mural is disturbed by applying the cinematic dispositif (Figure 2.7). The size as well as the position of the wall acquire the qualities of a screen upon which the—as if projected—image is set into motion by

Figure 2.7 Jan Šerých, *Kubrick's Carpet*, 2005. Dům U Kamenného zvonu, Prague. Courtesy of the artist.

the camera effect of an aggressive tracking in. Secondly, the mural is, in fact, not the "wall painting" (which is the official description that the gallery caption gives us) but rather an *unframed*, separated, and cut-out patterned "dismural" that creates a second-degree *parergon* of a kind. Both strategies, the media hybridity and spatial displacement, put the beholder into an uneasy encounter with the distorted, vertiginous perspective underlying the whole pattern composition through what the artist himself phrases as a "levitating point of view" (Císař 2008: x).

But how do these confusing patterns trigger the process of saturation and where does lie the site of ornamental excess? According to the visual theorist Karel Císař, the regular lines of Šerých's carpet design correspond to the hedge maze where the main protagonist of *The Shining*, the writer-turned-killer Jack Torrance, chases his son in the snow with the axe in hand, before freezing to death; both carpet patterns and labyrinthic twist thus mirror the descent into Jack's brain and his growing madness (2010: 38). As convincing as this observation certainly is, its emphasis on the narrative pretext of the painting overshadows the affective agency of the patterns that absorb the observing subject and follow the formal logic of ornament which is—since the frame was irreversibly broken—indifferent to its original source. To pursue the desubjectifying move of the painting, I would instead suggest that the core of its formal and affective work lies in the aforementioned troubling perspective that was reframed by and sifted through the digital technology. Once the carpet design is vertically placed on the cut-out mural, it becomes the wallpaper pattern that confuses the eye and forces the viewer to adapt a mobile perspective that is radically different than the human visual perception. For the eye, used to distinguishing a figure from its background, is watching nothing but at once moving and static geometric forms that are synchronically two- and three-dimensional.

So, just another exemplification of the current posthuman turn, one might easily conclude, but things are not that simple. Rather than "eliminat[ing] from his work any carnality or references to subjectivity" (Pospiszyl 2008: 49), in his "wallpaper painting" Šerých makes a more nuanced—and speculative at that—move by radically modifying the human and obviously embodied scopic regime according to the frozen and yet moving patterns. This step does not ultimately lead to removing the human subject altogether but to its absorption within the geometric framework of which it becomes a constitutive part. When the background is lost, an eye cannot rest for a single moment, and the accommodation becomes physically impossible, the subject has no other choice than to accept the rules of the ornamental—desubjectifying play of saturation. Pushing one step further Václav Magid's argument that "the perspective he [Šerých] brings, along with the position he manifests, is not human" (2008: 113), it can be concluded that this inhuman perspective is a result of the encounter and affective interaction between the unsettling patterns and the viewer whose capacity of looking is pushed to the limits.

Reinforced by the claustrophobic staging of this wallpaper right in front of a gallery wall, equally confusing are the outlined ornamental formations that emerge as a temporal illusion only to quickly disappear. Insofar as Šerých's painting forces us to constantly change perspective, we might occasionally discern an indication of a key—even though there is nothing to be opened or deciphered as precisely in Nabokov and Bergman—a surface of an electronic chip, a geometrically rendered design of the tiger fur, or the cryptic patterns of tropical butterflies. And this is where the insidious strategy of the painting lies: while in the wild nature such patterns serve to camouflage the animals' presence, Šerých's wallpaper hides nothing, constantly absorbing its beholding pray.

If the rococo engravings reveal the blending and mutual shaping of worlds inside and outside the frame and leave the representational regime in favor of performing their continual autoreferential movement, the modern literary and contemporary audiovisual mediations of the wallpaper patterns provide not so much a posthuman postscript to this art-historical chapter but rather a conceptual field, where the formal saturation and affective absorption are sustained through a specific rococo survival. There is a striking continuity between the excessive ornamental curves that once broke the frame to invade the pictorial space and the absorbing wallpaper patterns that reconfigure not only the surrounding space but also the subjects that happen to get too close. Without paying attention to the affective work of their forms, the wallpaper ornaments would remain just those innocent "free beauties," as the traditional aesthetics understands them until today.

Chapter 3

HOW TEXT BECOMES DIATEXT

GEMINI AND PERFORMATIVITY OF THE GARBAGE DUMP

What remains of people is what media can store and communicate.

Friedrich Kittler, *Gramophone, Film, Typewriter*, 1986

In the last but one part of her documentary film *Examined Life* (2008), director Astra Taylor follows one of its nine philosopher-protagonists, Slavoj Žižek, walking throughout a garbage dump in New York City, rummaging through discarded MC tapes and crumpled porn magazines while also inspecting a refrigerator full of the rotten food. With the wind ruffling his hair, characteristic turbulent gestures, and hasty articulation, Žižek explains to the camera that true love for the world consists in acknowledging trash and that the only proper way of facing the threat of ecological catastrophe is "that we should become more artificial."[1] In the midst of his explanation, however, his "trash message" is abruptly interrupted by the noise of and the subsequent camera track in to a truck dumping a heavy load of garbage on a heap, whereupon the so far spotlighted philosopher becomes derailed and his alluring discourse is thus not only short-circuited but also buried under the heavy mass of a noisy rubbish (Figure 3.1).

It would not be difficult to see in such an accidental, unintentional, and subversive agency of the matter—whose nonhuman and nonverbal "speech act" results into a purely disruptive perlocution that blocks both the discursive and visual stability of the talking subject—a confirmation of the new materialists' claim about the primacy of vibrant and agential matter.[2] Undoubtedly, the self-contained subject of the speaker becomes decentered here and the so far convincingly structured discourse is indeed substituted by an entirely different regime, the one of the alien objects emitting their own message. Yet there is much more to this scene, and as Kittler unpacks further his provocative claim standing for the epigraph to this chapter, the key force of media lies less in their

72 *Disformations*

Figure 3.1 A screen capture from Astra Taylor's *Examined Life* (2008). Zeitgeist Films. DVD.

messages and contents and more in their *circuits* that condition and enable their mediations (1999: xl–xli). In this particular circuit, it is not just mute yet boisterous objects and a talking subject who operate, but also a hardly noticeable anonymous driver who sets the garbage into motion, completely reframing the whole formal setting and subject-object network. As a result, the human subject neither disappears nor is eradicated by the disturbing agency of those refused objects but, instead, becomes a link within the operative chain and performative logic of the garbage—in other words, a medium.

That this event of being literally *drowned out* by garbage, whereby the human is no more a producer nor an analyst of the trash but rather a medium of its material, performative, and epistemic force, can have crucial consequences for thinking of both the affective and conceptual affordances of aesthetic forms, is tellingly demonstrated by Michel Tournier's 1975 novel *Gemini* (*Les Météores*), a text that can be read as a love letter to the once useful and then rejected forms that now strike back. First of all, the garbage dump here plays a pivotal role of the archaeological site where the main protagonist undertakes a hermeneutic of the collapsing civilization before and during the Second World War while reading this collapse through the human refuse. Secondly, as I will argue further, the novel revaluates the garbage forms by ultimately transforming the degraded waste material into a performative configuration that lays the ground for a novel media-theoretical concept, which I will call "diatext." By focusing on the encounter between the human subject and the garbage dump and their mutual mediality, this chapter explores how the affective operation of revaluation can turn a degraded material that seems good for nothing into a mode of performative thinking. Rather than analyzing the ways in which various waste products are represented as distinctive narrative objects, which is a dominant approach of the recent literary waste studies, I will investigate what media modalities and performative mechanisms drive the revaluation of garbage, what garbage *does* within the formal and affective work of the text, and how it forces us to think its aporetic logic of disformations.

Speaking for Rubbish: Tournier's Dandy Garbage Man versus Waste Studies

When Tournier published his 1975 novel *Gemini*, he was already a highly established author decorated with a number of prestigious literary awards, including Prix Goncourt that he received for his second and perhaps most famous novel *The Erl-King* (1970). Shortly after, Tournier becomes a member of the Gallimard readers' committee and the combination of his position as a writer, whose prose and essays have been world bestsellers until today, and the direct participation in literary life have made him for several decades not only "one of the most bankable European novelists" (Worton 2014: 11) but also one of the leading voices of the French postmodern writing. In this light, *Gemini* can be read both as an experimental step into a less charted territory of metafiction, where the self-disclosed narrator becomes a part of the metaleptic mise en abyme game (as suggested by the very first page of the novel displaying a mirror image of the author himself, reading on a beach Aristotle's treatise *Meteorologica*), and as a comeback of a raw, materialist realism wherein the so far dominant mythical symbolism pervading historical events is disenchanted on a garbage dump heaping up the trash, filth, and corpses. None of these readings would be wrong—unless a narrative thematic and an allegorical representation were the main novel's concerns.

The novel has two interconnected, albeit mostly independent, parts differing at the level of storytelling, style, and spatiotemporal coordinates. The first part recounts the story of Jean-Paul's "geminate cell," the monozygotic twin brothers growing up before the Second World War within the environment of the family textile factory surrounded by an idyllic Breton landscape. Since their earliest childhood, they have been indulging in an incestuous relationship while communicating by means of a secret, mysterious-sounding, and encrypted "Aeolian" language; but as they grow up, the twins' irreconcilably different characters become manifest, as metaphorically laid out in their nicknames of Carder-Jean and Warper-Paul. In his attempt to break the bond of the "ovoid loving" and to escape what he calls the "geminate prison," Jean sets on a journey around the world, being relentlessly pursued by Paul from Venice to Djerba, across Iceland to Japan and Vancouver to finally—as if to mirror the cracking gemini bond—end up in postwar Berlin, which is just being divided by the Wall. While the story of the twins, underlaid by a continual passing and separation, forms a larger part of the novel, it also received more critical attention focused dominantly on its reinvigorated myth of Dioscuri (the mythical twin-sons of Leda), thematic variations of the initiation and incest as well as on the metafictional link between the celestial elements and the main protagonists' fate.[3]

In what follows, however, I will delve uniquely into the second part of the novel, structured around the homoerotic escapades and philosophical reflections of the geminis' uncle Alexandre who, roughly aged twenty and by a lucky accident of his petty-bourgeois brother Gustave's sudden death, becomes the owner and manager of a company in charge of six garbage dumps in Rennes, Deauville, Paris, Marseilles, Roanne, and Casablanca. The encounter with these giant waste yards quickly transforms Alexandre's entire life, turning a mere "shocking uncle" and a libertine dandy into the "king of garbage men," a self-proclaimed ruler of an empire of waste. Besides depicting love affairs and sexual adventures, his narration is grounded in the extensive reflections on absurdity of the omnipresent binary arrangement of the human society with its rigid interpersonal relations, and focalized through a prism of the garbage dump that accumulates, stores, and transforms the almost mummified and only slowly degrading waste, one that is discarded by the normative society he despises.

Although Tournier's *Gemini* elaborated his tried-and-tested aesthetics of combining mythopoetic tropes and philosophical fragments with an overarching eroticism while joyfully tackling various sexual taboos, the book garnered a mixed and mostly negative critical response. Curiously, it even received criticism from the author himself who labeled it, in retrospect, as "compositionally unbalanced," primarily due to his personal enchantment with the figure of Alexandre who was originally supposed to be a rather secondary character.[4] In short, Tournier was scolded for obscenity, blasphemy, and vitriolic attack on heterosexuality in favor of a plea for homosexuality.[5] One exemplary response was given by a then respected critic, Robert Kanters, who in his 1975 review of the book for *Le Figaro littéraire* refused to quote a certain scatological and mockingly anti-heterosexual passage from the novel "unless this newspaper were printed on toilet paper" and wished that the book would be "flung on one of those rubbish dumps to which the author is so attracted" (Bracker 2001: 72).[6] In contrast to this judgment that deemed Tournier's book "hollow and full of filth [creux et plein d'ordures]," I want to argue that the novel challenges us to take that "filth" out of the axiology and illuminate it from the perspective of its performativity that generates not only aesthetic formations but also theoretical concepts.

To do so, it is crucial to note that the initial encounter between the main protagonist and the universe of garbage happens through nothing else but the medium of text. Despite his fundamental resistance to any useful activity, especially the one of taking over his brother's landfill business, Alexandre unexpectedly finds himself fully absorbed by reading the company's memorandum, entitled "TURDCO and its Task of Repurgation." It is this short document—whose French acronym of the company's name (*SEDOMU: Société d'enlèvement des ordures ménagères urbaines*), uncovers a homophonic pun interlinking sodomy with waste—that triggers the protagonist's affective bond with the realm of the garbage, so much so that it will soon have turned his previous life upside down.

> Repurgation! The word might have come out of a medical treatise on the digestive system or a study of theological casuistry. That neologism—no use looking it up in any dictionary—was Gustave all over in the way it conveyed his attempt to make up for his horrible calling by putting on airs of intestino-spiritual research. But what did I not learn on that night of September 26–27, 1934, a night only to be compared with that of the great Pascal's nocturnal phantasy! (Tournier 1998: 28)

No matter if the narrator calls the protagonist "king of garbage men," depicts him as a charming sovereign libertine or presents him as an eloquent garbage philosopher, the combination of aristocratic pride and the obsession with all kinds of trash, litter, waste, and junk creates a dominant perspective of the novel, in the light of which even the most repulsive and hardly nameable waste is methodically elevated to a sacred fetish, which, in turn, translates the very subject into an extravagant garbage configuration. This is visible, for instance, when Alexandre wears six gold medallions on his embroidered silk waistcoats, each of them containing "a compressed sample of the refuse of its own city." For the "dandy garbage man," these rubbish ornaments immediately become a formative tool of his own metamorphosis: "And thus hung about with relics, transformed into a refuse reliquary, armed with the sixfold seal of his secret empire, the emperor of dust should go forth to promenade the world" (29). While these frequent games, disguises, and self-creations, driven by an eccentric mixture of flamboyance, swashbuckling, and grotesque imagination, play out the protagonist's self-reflected double position of being both the subject and a highly artificial object, the discourse of the novel does not cease to underscore that this perspective is produced by, through, and with garbage. Rather than investing the protagonist with a symbolic meaning and expression, the text thus opens up a possibility of reading this subject as *a relay* whose primary agency is being the medium of this peculiar object constellation—a reading not so much against the grain, but rather a *reading with the waste.*

To be sure, this is a different theoretical move than the one which would follow an increasing scholarly interest in the phenomenon and cultural practices of garbage, going over the past two decades under the transdisciplinary label of waste studies and exploring all kinds of material refusals through the lens of archaeology, sociology, cultural anthropology, environmental studies, but also as a source of art production.[7] Leaving aside the recent debates of whether it would be more appropriate to talk about "discard studies" rather than "waste studies" (Liboiron 2014)—and thus the very problem of the semantic distinction between trash, waste, and garbage—it almost seems that the ongoing "material-cultural turn" (Hicks 2010) emphasizing not only the matter, objects, or things that mankind produces but also the one it refuses and discards has gained one more paradigmatic spin that might be dubbed a "garbage turn."[8]

Whatever types of waste products scholars focus on—be they described as refuse, litter, detritus, scrap, rubbish, trash, junk, or simply leftovers—they all recognize garbage as a productive cluster of objects, elements, and phenomena that due to their transitional and hybrid nature—and for all our inclination to cast them aside—can help us better understand and interpret the human practices, rituals, and even ways of thinking. While the "waste and garbage are both irreducibly material yet culturally constructed and economically determined" (Foote and Mazzolini 2012: 9), the rationale for this positive stance can be also found in the ontological proximity between humans and waste, the former of which at once condition and are conditioned by the latter. No matter whether we trash a useless thing, a fragment of the past or a disturbing memory, they will always return to us in their renewed physical and symbolical forms. Such is also a framing argument of John Scanlan's inspiring work on how Western culture understands and deals with the universe of garbage, suggesting that the returning "spectres of garbage serve as a stark reminder of what we really are" (2005: 12).

A similar perspective is taken up by the recent scholarship that applies waste studies into the approaches of cultural analysis and literary studies.[9] Far from merely "scavenging familiar textual landfills," to borrow a nifty phrase from Susan Signe Morrison (2015: 5), this field examines both the discourse and practices of the "textual waste" (Viney 2014: 79) ranging from the Middle Ages to the present day, exploring essentially two main domains: the ways the garbage and waste are represented, narrated, and symbolized and functional analogies between the garbage techniques such as recycling, composting, reuse, and literary intertextual strategies.[10] In contrast, I wish to pursue a different direction and instead of asking how waste and garbage are represented in the sense of narrative and visual objects and in what ways they enter an intertextual dialogue, I argue for the garbage dump as a figural site of disformations whose performative mediality is possible only through the affective encounter with and by reproducing the operational mechanisms of garbage.[11]

The Media Archaeology of Garbage

Through the lens of Alexandre, the garbage dump operates as both the place of fascination and generator of a new, inverted, and playfully perverse logic. While underlying the basic narrative infrastructure and conceptual framework of the whole novel, the dump also reinforces the protagonist's libertine and homoerotic position that is not merely sexual but primarily hermeneutic, although it is almost constantly disrupted by self-irony.[12] At the same time, the garbage dump constitutes for him a mirror site of identification, given by the fact that "[a] society defines itself by what it throws away—which instantly becomes an absolute—domestic refuse and homosexuals in particular" (Tournier 1998: 170). Rather than relying on any stable ontology, let alone politics, of this repudiated identity, the analogy between the protagonist and the rubbish site builds upon its dynamic of forms, traces, events, and negation: "A collection of signatures and celebrations, emptiness, absurdity and absolute—in these characteristic elements of my natural environment, I well recognize the constants of my mind and heart" (248). Even though his eloquent dandyism and perpetual self-exposure could imply otherwise, the novel replaces a self-contained, autonomous, postromantic subject with a flamboyant medium of the garbage network of which it makes a constitutive part.

Not from outside but from within this garbage network does *Gemini* manifest Alexandre's hermeneutic position, inasmuch as his official job—which is to ensure that waste be "preserved indefinitely in a dry and sterile medium [milieu] by means of controlled dumping" (75–6)—is but an excuse to fully succumb to its semantic, affective, and media polyphony. In the garbage, leftovers, and filth, the protagonist reads the traces of historical events, conducts an archaeological research of the contemporary civilization, and bears witness to it. To close this not just hermeneutic but also mimetic circle, the protagonist's testimony is ultimately silenced around a garbage dump where he is murdered like a stray dog. It is as if, through his trashing agency, the Old Testament aphorism "For you are dust and to dust you shall return" were translated into a materialist, consumer logic which places both the origin and destiny into their wasteful nature.

> Little by little I began to be attracted by the negative, I might almost say *inverted* aspect of this industry. Certainly it was an empire that spread through city streets and had its country acres—the dumps—also; but equally it penetrated into people's most intimate secrets, since every deed and every action left its mark on it, the irrefutable proof of its doing—cigarette butts, torn-up letters, vegetable peelings, sanitary napkins, and so forth. In fact, it was a complete takeover of a whole community, and a takeover that came from behind, from the rear, reversed and nocturnal. (28–9)

Such inverted perspective enables the text a step toward a daring anachronism which makes a garbage heap no more a lifeless pile of the past remnants and refusals but instead a highly potent "site for archaeological excavation, but a very special one because it concerns the archaeology of the present" (170). Less than in the manner of the Foucaultian archaeology of knowledge undertaken through the archives that tacitly prioritizes the written language, Tournier's archaeology of the present is invested in the mediality—connections, links, and circuits—of the trashed materials and objects, making a valuable interlocutor to the current media philosophers who shift the focus of media theory from the fixed communication objects to the media "processes, transformations, and events" (Horn 2007: 8). Structured around the plea for a subversive agency of trash, with which Alexandre identifies and that is frequently depicted with a tone of love lyricism, the novel delineates the garbage dump as a conceptual field enabling a systematic reflection of contemporary civilization from the point of view of what and how this civilization refuses, discards, suppress. Thanks to the garbage dump, whose mediator the protagonist is, the human element of the entire garbage network becomes not only a voyeur but also an archaeologist and semiotician of society. Curiously enough, his attempt to take over society "from behind" is anything but a mere literary invention. So let us pause here for a moment on a cultural practice whose methods shed some light on the novel's revaluation of the seemingly worthless garbage forms.

In response to an increasingly problematic storage of domestic waste in the United States, in 1973 (only two years before the publication of Tournier's novel), a collective scholarly "Garbage Project" involving hundreds of students and dozens of participating organizations was founded at the University of Arizona in Tucson under the guidance of the archaeologist William Rathje. Successful in its goal to investigate the community trash of some 15,000 households through a sample of around 125 tons of garbage and thus to map consumption of food, drugs, sanitation items, pet-related products and also piles of old newspapers, the project quickly led to a discipline known as garbology, one that attempted to understand consumer waste as both an object of archaeological research and a precious source of anthropologic knowledge about contemporary civilization. From its standpoint, the garbage dump embodies a fruitful place where various events, objects, and rituals accumulate and which can, in turn, be classified, deciphered, and interpreted. To make their case, garbologists advocate the idea of waste being one of the most productive sources of information on the character, habits, and practices of human society, and even more significant than statistical data based on industrial production, sales of goods, and consumer reports (Rathje and Murphy 2001: 54).[13]

Not only do the funding premises of garbology that "there is a garbage angle to every human activity" and that "the creation of garbage is an unequivocal sign of a human presence" (Rathje and Murphy 2001: 9) clearly resonate with the meanings assigned to those remnants of civilization by *Gemini* but despite their contrasting—scholarly versus aesthetic—regimes of the knowledge production, the former and the latter also set themselves a common speculative and, for that matter, topographical goal. While the novel calls for an insolent inquiry into the society "from behind, from the rear, reversed and nocturnal" (28–29), the garbological aim is "to investigate human behavior 'from the back end'" (Rathje and Murphy 2001: 14).[14] Alexandre's exploration of the rubbish and the scientific garbological research do not meet just in their basic consumer notion of the human as a permanent generator of the "valuable" rubbish but also in the affective alliance with the material and semiotic qualities of the dump—so much so that both the aesthetic and theoretical qualities of the garbage lay the ground for an affective operation of the revaluation of its forms. Accordingly, both the fictional and real garbologists articulate their materialist joy, curiosity, and hermeneutic desire in face of the body of the rubbish to such an extent that their discourse is interchangeable at places:

> To understand garbage you have to touch it, to feel it, to sort it, to smell it. You have to pick through hundreds of tons of it, counting and weighing all the daily newspapers, the telephone books; the soiled diapers, the foam clamshells that once briefly held hamburgers, the lipstick cylinders coated with grease, the medicine vials still encasing brightly colored pills, the empty bottles of scotch, the half-full cans of paint and muddy turpentine, the forsaken toys, the cigarette butts. (Rathje and Murphy 2001: 9)

But is it really? What ties together the practices of garbology and Alexandre's "reversed" archaeology is not only the hermeneutic understanding of the waste material, providing a positive source of knowledge about the past and present times, but also an aesthetic judgment related to a specific corporeal stance. Instead of provoking the Kantian disgust that Brinkema elegantly rephrases as "an unintegratable aspect of the aesthetic that the aesthetic cannot speak" (2014: 126), such a stance triggers the affect of curiosity and enhances engagement of bodily senses that nuance and classify a whole of the refuse. Yet what seems unquestionable from the materialist point of view subscribing to the corporeal and sensory engagement with the matter under the archaeological scrutiny, from the mediaphilosophical perspective framing the present inquiry these aesthetic views become conceptually productive only when the Cartesian inquiring subject—the garbologist, that is—becomes decentered in favor of its functional position within an operative chain linking the humans and objects, one that radically complicates any assumptions about their ontological divisibility. Only then the garbage dump ceases to be a passive reservoir of meanings and representations indifferently waiting to be excavated and explained to finally become a dynamic media configuration grounded in the way "it activates our senses, our reflexivity, and our practices" (Casetti 2015: 5). Through the protagonist's careful reading and subsequent application of the discursive and material mediations of the garbage, the novel shifts a traditional hermeneutics of the trash into a *performative thinking with the trash* that produces aesthetic forms and concepts.

In order for the garbage forms to be revaluated and illuminated in their aesthetic and conceptual performativity, these forms need to generate a novel thinking which expands on the formal qualities of trash. *Gemini* plays out this compelling step by means of an analogy between the formal composition of the garbage dump and the organ of thought, suggesting that "this fibrous substance with pearly lights in it has a certain affinity with the intricate synaptic substance of the human brain. Roanne, city of cerebral rubbish!" (Tournier 1998: 73). Far from providing a mere autotelic metaphor based on the visual similarity between the center of the nervous system and "this pinkish-gray waste, dense, rich and thickly felted by the wool shoddy" (72–3), the text surpasses a mimetic representation en route to *imitate* the formal movement of the garbage dump driven by its material and organic excess. In doing so, this metaphor of "cerebral rubbish" becomes immediately a conceptual figure that is materialized into a specific object which unfolds the epistemic force of the dump, yielding a knowledge in the form of old books that emerge as "the inevitable flora of this intelligent midden, these ciphers; they have grown on it like mushrooms, they are their sublimated emanation" (73). Creating both the aesthetically and epistemically fertile ground, engendering new dynamic forms endowed with memory and knowledge, the garbage dump carries out its material thinking with the rubbish through the medium of text—a thinking one might phrase as a performance through imitation.

Reading a Figure, Trashing the Subject

The so far multifarious and playfully subversive "back end" has, however, its dark side, unfolding through a tragic note that continually takes over the whole narrative. Immediately before and during the raging war, Alexandre travels between his cherished city dumps, on one occasion accidentally encountering in Paris Hitler himself (whom he quickly labels as "Chancellor Adolf Heterosexual"; 1998: 244), only to end his life tragically in the proximity of a garbage dump in Casablanca. The initially frolicsome episodes, which cover mostly erotic reminiscences from adolescence, adventures with the members of "the ragpicking fraternity" and pursuing his desired "quarry" at city dumps and in the nocturnal parks, give continually way to sinister events as the Second World War draws near. Foreshadowed by an apocalyptic scene in which seagulls and rats fight it out at a giant dump in southwest France, whose towering heaps are constantly dispersed by the mistral, and during which Alexandre's lover Daniel is mauled to death by rats, it soon becomes clear that along with the archaeological site accumulating all kinds of trash, rubbish, waste, and litter, the garbage dump works also as a generator of prophetic images.[15]

Hence, the imminent war comes to the protagonist not only through the clusters of an inanimate waste but also in the form of real corpses. At one point, after the exodus of the French from the capital, a train of thirty-five wagons brings thousands of dog carcasses decimated by German soldiers to the wide plains of the Parisian dumps. Later on, during the weeks of truce, the rotting remains of fine pastries, decaying smoked meats, reeking dairy products, and heaps of putrefying flowers are also dumped (246–9). Prefigured by the transport of dead animals, the apocalyptic vision of the country's decline and the war massacre is thus crowned by the image of leftovers pouring toward Alexandre after the Parisians return to their homes and reopen their businesses. "This time," Alexandre sums up right before his voluntary death in Casablanca, "this fearsome vomit, this puke that stinks to heaven, is a fair and terrible warning of the depths to which Paris and France will sink beneath the invader's heel" (249). Within this peculiar semiotics of garbage, the present traces not only refer to the recent past but also become indexes of the dreadful future.

> The summer is ending and there is the threat of war. Hitler, having completed the massacre of German homosexuals with the connivance of the world at large, is seeking further victims. Need I say that the massive heterosexual conflict which is brewing interests me as an onlooker, but is no concern of mine? Except that perhaps for the last act, when Europe and the whole world will probably be reduced to a single heap of rubble. (187)

At first glance, investigating the human society through what it refuses can lead to a modernist diagnosis of the civilization on the brink of its historical collapse. For that matter, the garbage dump is elevated to the level of a historical figure, or, more precisely, to *figura*, which Erich Auerbach in his 1938 essay explains as a rhetorical structure operating within historiography, that is equally important for its current representation and anticipation. Insofar as the *figura* means "something real and historical which announces something else that is also real and historical," it is endowed with memory of the past while revealing a future temporality because establishing "a connection between two events or persons, the first of which signifies not only itself but also the second, while the second encompasses or fulfills the first" (Auerbach 1984: 29, 53).[16]

It is precisely this figural reading of the garbage dump which allows the novel's garbologist to pursue the parallel between the destruction of a useless trash and the holocaust: "A strange, prophetic analogy! At the very moment we are talking of burning garbage, sinister rumors are coming out of Germany that Adolf Hitler is making his own arrangements" (Tournier 1998: 87). What the novel describes as a forecast of an apocalypse, fragments of a historical tragedy, traces of war rage, and indices of transports leaves no doubt in the mind of the protagonist, who reads all these indications through the lens of the garbage to finally conjure up the prophetic vision of genocide—another word for a mass liquidation of those who are seen (by those in power) as a "human rubbish." However, whereas the classical diagnosis consists in a self-distanced identification of a disease from its signs and symptoms, *Gemini* does the labor of diagnosis without this ethical distance. As a result, it comes closer to its etymological root of the Greek *diagignōskein* (*OED*, s.v. "diagnosis"), which indicates that to know, to learn, to perceive (*gignōskein*) should come in the direction of "through" (*dia*) and not just "from" or "about"—and hence turns the fatality of the figural reading of the garbage onto the protagonist-reader himself, ending his life on the garbage dump. The figural reading thus has a capacity to undermine the traditional diagnosis; instead of being distinguished from those catastrophic signs and war traces, the destructive logic of the trash is performed *through* and *from within* them. If the fundamental paradox of the waste lies in that it "might indeed suggest a sense of temporal disruption, but it is also matter that lingers and remains" (Viney 2014: 16), to mediate this temporal paradox the subject needs to trash itself.

The historical and, by the same token, political figurality of the garbage dump can easily be traced beyond the fictional France during the Second World War, for instance to the Central-East European context, where it was tellingly used by the Czech director Jiří Menzel in his film *Larks on a String (Skřivánci na niti*, 1969). Set in the totalitarian

Czechoslovakia of the early 1950s, the film places a scrap heap as the central memorial site of the era before the communist regime which, at the same time, adumbrates the forthcoming Stalinist repression. "Class enemies" are forced to expiate their bourgeois origins at a metal scrap processing plant, where, just as scrap is "smelted down into high-grade steel," they are also to be transformed into a more useful material. As announced by the head of the plant: "We'll make tractors from this steel to plough our fields and more washers so you can wash your overalls. These are our volunteer workers, mostly of bourgeois origin. We'll also smelt them down into a new kind of people."[17] In addition to this quite a transparent critique of the communist ideology, the film, which began shooting during the Prague Spring of 1968 and was completed only after the invasion of the Soviet army, plays out a crucial media-historical moment: a crane dumping old typewriters into giant containers so that they, too, are reforged into "more useful" machines (Figure 3.2). While this scene prefigures—on the level of diegesis—the real official ban of hundreds of writers along with destruction of their texts across the former Soviet bloc, it also reveals a peculiar mise en abyme recursion since Menzel's film was—exactly as the diegetic trash—banned and "discarded" immediately after its release, and made it to cinemas only one year after the fall of the Iron Curtain in 1989.

Figure 3.2 A screen capture from Jiří Menzel's *Larks on a String* (1969). Bontonfilm, 2005. DVD.

As media artists and scholars tell us, the trashed "materials also come into existence as a force when the political, geographical and economic situations are right for them to do so" (Fuller 2010; qtd. in Parikka 2015: 104). Notably, the intermingling of the human and nonhuman elements that is both a prerequisite and a tangible result of any garbage configuration shows that this force is not necessarily favorable to humans and that it is poised to a mutual wasting and destruction. However, the novel is a far cry from falling into a moral judgment of such a negativity, arguing instead— in a very Bataillean manner—for an excessive economy of wasting.

> Middle-class cheeseparing! Always terrified to throw anything away, like a miser hating to let go of anything. With one obsession, one ideal: a society in which *nothing* would be ever thrown away, where things would last forever and where the two great processes of production and consumption would be carried on with no waste at all! It's the dream of a completely constipated city. Whereas what I dream of is an entirely disposable world where a whole city could be thrown on the scrap heap. But isn't that just what we are promised in the next war, with the aerial bombing they say we shall have? (68)

And this is where the modernist diagnosis, putting an insurmountable barrier between the Cartesian subject and its material "other," is turned upside down. Not only does the protagonist's thinking, driven by the desire for an absolute waste, allow to view the economy of the imminent war as both destructive and generative but, more importantly, the novel's revaluation of the garbage forms also is made literal and ultimately materialized by a spectacular trashing of Alexandre's own life. Navigating his dream of "an entirely disposable world" inward himself, he sets out on a final night-time hunt in Casablanca, dressed in an elegant embroidered vest and stone broke: "What was the stranger's advice about the docks? No jewels, no weapons and some ready money? Then I shall not take a sou. Fleurette shall be on my arm and in my ears shall shine the Philippine pearls" (276). The media logic of this suicidal act could not be sharper: the subject has to withdraw so that the garbage gets its voice. And if the dialectic mechanism of the trash is such that it "consumes its own being" (Kennedy: 162), to revaluate this logic of negation one needs to *reproduce it*. By reproducing the disposable nature of the garbage through the body of the subject which thus becomes a relay of its logic, the novel rewrites what Bataille called the "nonproductive expenditure," including those useless or destructive activities that "have no end beyond themselves" (1988: 118), into a productive wasting.[18]

From Metatext to Diatext

Let us now return to the central moment of the novel, that is the
encounter of the subject with the garbage, and to the way the affective
relationship to the garbage forms activate a new kind of mediation.
While Michael Worton calls Alexandre the most logical of Tournier's
perverts (2014: 21), it should be specified that his logic of perversion is
grounded less in an independent will of the self-centered subject and
more in the reproduction of the inversive mechanisms structuring and
sustaining the garbage dump. The key operations of the latter include
a perpetual emptying of the old content and original matter and the
loss of its initial purpose through what the novel sets out as "the
filter of consumption" that leads to the complete desubjectification of
the garbage.

> What is left is the empty bottle, the squeezed tube, the orange
> peel, the chicken bones, the hard, durable parts of the product, the
> elements of the inheritance which our civilization will bequeath to
> the archaeologists of the future. [. . .] Not without getting my own
> excitement, before their inhumation, from the infinite repetition
> of these mass-produced objects—the copies of copies of copies of
> copies of copies of copies and so on. (75–6)[19]

In this final chant of the key term, Tournier, a master of manifold
intertextual allusions, may be either simply improvising or, more
likely given his deep knowledge of the contemporary French
philosophy, playfully alluding to a no less complex imitation. At one
point in his *Difference and Repetition* (1968), Tournier's close friend
and philosophical mentor Deleuze paraphrases Pierre Klossowski's
argument explaining Nietzsche's concept of the eternal return, holding
that "each thing exists only in returning, copy of an infinity of copies
which allows neither original nor origin to subsist" (2004: 80).
Therefore, it seems justified to suggest that this very multiplication and
self-mirroring of the anonymous copies without origin lie at heart of
Tournier's logic of repetition.[20]

It would be tempting to read *Gemini*'s celebration of copies and
permanently commented analogies as a postmodernist declaration
par excellence, pleading for an autoreferential entropy of repetitions,
reproductions, and self-mirroring allusions and imitations. Such a reading
would clearly correspond to Jameson's assertion that all cultural forms
of postmodernism are characterized by pastiche, in the sense of various

stylistic and intertextual borrowings, imitations, and combinations, and to his emphasis on reproduction prevailing over innovation as "the deepest subject" of all postmodernism (1991: 17–25, 95). In this view, the text of the novel would figure as an instance of a *metatextual play*, which is precisely a reading provided by a thorough study of Nicole Bracker who argues that "[t]he garbage heap becomes a symbol of Tournier's palimpsestic rewritings in which various versions of the same text are repeated and heaped up upon an absent original, disrupting any notion of a unified aesthetic object," while the waste in the novel would eventually function "as a metatextual metaphor concerning author, reader and text" (2001: 67, 72). But such a cogent observation raises the question as to what new understanding can this metadiscursive reading bring not only about a novel's specific work of forms but also about literary language in general. Why should we vigorously ransack through the textual garbage only to find out that this garbage refers to something beyond the text, something that was already here and that we knew in advance? Something important goes missing when we rely too much on the distinction between a text's— or any medium's, for that matter—showing and telling, and this something is nothing less than its performativity *qua* what the text does with and what is done to it through the very forms it accumulates.

For what is piled up on the garbage heap are not a few innocent metaphors but a formal inversion which thwarts at once a narrative hierarchy and any meaningful distinction between objects, subjects, and their forms: "After the substance has melted away, the form itself becomes substance. Hence the incomparable richness of this pseudo-substance which is nothing but an accumulation of forms" (Tournier 1998: 248). When taken seriously, the conceptual trajectory of this inversion exceeds by far the intentional metatextual strategy on the way to generating a singular textual modality, one that takes up the *work of wasting*.

At the very beginning of the chapter entitled "Aesthetic of the Dandy Garbage Man," this inversion emerges fully fledged as a well-round tautological circle:

> The idea is more than the thing and the idea of the idea more than the idea. Wherefore the imitation is more than the thing imitated, because it is the thing plus the effort of imitation, which incorporates the possibility of reproducing itself, and so of adding quantity to quality. (74)

Enabled by the logic of the dump, this anti-essentialist axiology is voiced by none other than Alexandre, who, in his swashbuckling tone and wielding a swordstick, instead of the Nietzschean hammer, shatters the foundation stones of continental philosophy. And he does so boldly, as this plea for copies and imitations turns his aesthetic creed into a manifesto of anti-Platonism, radically reverting the platonic doctrine of artistic imitation.[21] According to Plato, as we read in Socrates' dialogue with Glaucon in the tenth book of his *Republic*, imitation—*mimesis*— is always an inferior activity, since it only imperfectly reproduces the original, that is, the primordial immaterial idea (2004: 297–326). While Plato rejects the imitation as an "inferior thing that consorts with another inferior thing to produce inferior offspring," (2004: 307) such as works of art that are but worthless copies of copies, the novel extols any imitated thing as "the original encapsulated, possessed, integrated and even multiplied—in short, considered and spiritualized" (Tournier 1998: 74). To make this logic of the self-reproducing imitation work, it is not enough to symbolically represent all those accumulated garbage forms but instead to exploit and reduplicate them within the discursive structure of the text that organizes these forms.

The proliferation of copies makes possible an analogical nature of the garbage dump that penetrates the whole narrative while shaping the affective process of revaluation. So when the protagonist during one of his erotic hunts discovers that his desired prey is being pursued by another hunter-predator, we are presented an analogical reading of this situation as hunting "the quarry of the quarry," which is nothing but "the erotic equivalent of the idea of the idea, the copy of the copy" (Tournier 1998: 79). The affective logic of the erotic desire and the performative logic of the dump based on reproductions and imitations are thoroughly attuned. In other words, the subject *repeats* what the garbage *does* and in the same way the garbage dump melts a preexisting substance away, the narrative strips away its metaphysical baggage through the incessant and repetitive self-explanations. As a result, these permanently commented analogies lead to nothing but a structural analogy between the diegetic self-reflection *within* the text and the performative thinking *of* the text.

Rather than placing this self-reflective language into the well charted territory of metatext, I want to argue that this kind of discourse *imitates* the process of consumption to reproduce the mechanism and logic of the garbage dump. All those continuous comments, analogies, and explanations of the protagonist's actions and thoughts do exactly what the "filter of consumption" does to the objects that end up on the garbage dump. Pushing the representational regime toward the infinite copies and repetitions, the novel wastes, squanders, and hollows out both its diegesis and reflections. The performative mechanisms and techniques of the garbage dump are thus faithfully imitated by a self-referential discourse which lays bare, empties, sifts, and filters the narrative coordinates of the novel through the filter of commentary. If the waste is what informs the discourse of a text, one should read with it and not against or beyond it. But how to read something that trashes itself?

My indication that the formal work of the text discloses something more than a metatextual strategy requires a venture into a different and perhaps a less self-evident vocabulary. In order to underscore a performative potential of the self-referential discourse, I would like to offer a term that substitutes the spatiotemporal and discursive distance of the prefix *meta*—in the sense of "above," "over," "beyond," or "trans"— with another prefix which would denote a direct presence, synchronous activity, and mutual operationality of both the diegetic and conceptual levels. According to Dieter Mersch, this function is taken up by the Greek prefix *dia* which denotes (in the sense of the Latin *per*) "through," "in," and "by means of." Unlike the too strict semantics of *meta* which "always implies that a boundary has to be crossed" (for instance, in the Greek word for metaphor: *meta-pherein*) and refers etymologically to a clear transition or "the act of a leap" between two disparate places, the dynamic agency and semantic topography of the preposition *dia* shifts the attention from fixed objects and media to the very act of mediality (Mersch 2016: 665). "Whereas *meta, trans* or *über* (over) refer to a transfer or transmission whose basis remains questionable, various ways or modalities of ensuring transition are indicated by *dia* or *per*" (668). Since *Gemini* shows conspicuously that comments, self-reflection, and sustained autoreferentiality do not assume a distant position toward diegesis and narrative strategies but are rather enacted *through* them—just as the diegetic world is precisely enacted *through* and by means of the commentary—it seems useful to take this two-way mediality into account and name this type of performative discourse a "dia-text." Merging the alleged boundaries between representation and exegesis and enabling their mutual reshaping, the media operation of *diatext* shows the possibility of a text being structured by the very forms it accumulates.

The fact that the simultaneously self-emptying and self-generating movement of the garbage penetrates the very texture of the novel has a significant implication for the mediality of both the garbage dump and the subject. For if the novel stages the garbage as a "pseudo-substance" within which any original substance is immediately replaced by an infinite chain of copies, and the self-voiding mechanism of which is continually extended, reproduced, and mediated by the protagonist, then he, too, loses any autonomy and becomes just one among other garbage objects. However, if the present reading with the waste avoided the temptation to read *Gemini* in the light of a postmodern metatextual play, one should not succumb to an equally justifiable yet no less hasty temptation to read the novel as a forerunner of speculative realism. Certainly, *Gemini* helps to explore what object-oriented ontology posits as "countless layers of withdrawn real things" (Harman 2009: 215) and shows them as independent to the human will to such an extent that they may be harmful or even destructive to them. But unlike Harman's claim that "[r]eal objects withdraw from all human access and even from causal interaction with each other" (2012: 188)—which necessarily maintains the Cartesian dualism of objects and subjects—*Gemini* makes a more compelling theoretical move in that it actually short-circuits this opposition. Not by a naïve rejection or elimination of the human agency as such, but rather by *turning an autonomous subject into the medium of objects.*[22]

If the form becomes substance because the substance itself has melted away, the formal reading subscribing to the logic of generative disturbances has no other choice than to follow this paradox into its theoretical consequences. It is of little importance whether the affective operation of revaluation of the garbage proceeds intentionally or not; what matters is to allow the accumulation of rejected and allegedly useless forms to perform their inverted logic of disformations within a text, be it a film text as was the case with both Žižek's interrupted post-humanist message and Menzel's recursive scrap heaps, or the literary text as in *Gemini*, wherein the protagonist undertakes the archaeology of civilization by tackling its refuse in the twilight of modernism. Only then can the garbage, whose constant motion of forms triggers both disarray and fascination, become a conceptual force that not only is represented in the text but also gives its discourse the structure of, what I tried to argue for as, the "diatext." A heap of infinite trash as well as a reservoir of semiotic traces, a buried anonymous rubbish as well as new forms rid of old content, an archaeological site as well as a place teeming with wasted yet manifold forms and their random configurations—the garbage dump is all that but it is also a site of powerful mediations that opens up aesthetic and conceptual avenues for rethinking those forms we could wrongly consider useless.

Chapter 4

THE PORTRAIT OF ABSENCE,
OR WHEN THE EMPTY CHAIRS GET CROWDED

In point of fact, all the portrait ever does is manifest approximate
allures of absence.

Jean-Luc Nancy, *The Look of the Portrait*, 2000

Is it possible to capture an absence of the human subject by means of
a portrait? Or is it even necessary, since the presence of an absence, as
suggested by Belting (2011: 6), is both an inherent feature and a founding
paradox of any image? Over the past two decades, the voices of art
historians might have indicated that the genre of portraiture is now long
gone. Such a skepticism is especially sound in relation to the present era
of a "digital masquerade" wherein, according to Belting's diagnosis, we
become surrounded by artificially generated or biotechnically morphed
"cyberfaces" that completely undermine ideas of facial resemblance and
likeness and that "are not faces but rather digital masks with which the
production of faces has reached a turning point in the modern media"
(2017: 239, 241). But as soon as we change the angle and see the portrait
not as a constitutional, albeit somewhat obsolete, genre that has been
crucial for the articulation of modern individuality but rather as a media
operation that instead of representing the portrayed subjects *performs*
them, the portrait seems to be alive and well. This kind of performance,
I would wager, has a capacity to shift the negativity of an absent subject
into a generative lack, a lack that stages and informs the presence of a
missing subject via its tangible absence. In other words, to capture an
absence of the subject the portrait can undertake a *swap* that decenters
and replaces the subject en route to give shape to its affective trace, to
permanently provoke a desire for its presence, to see it coming without
having it ever come.

Drawing on the paintings of Francis Bacon, Lucien Freud, Marlene
Dumas and staged photography by Cindy Sherman, van Alphen
argues that unlike the classical portrait, whose aim was to render

the authority of the subject, in the twentieth century, the genre of portraiture returned in order "to show a loss of self instead of its consolidation, to shape the subject as simulacrum instead of as origin" (2005: 25). In a similar vein and to explain how many of modernist and contemporary visual artists underscore removal or deformation of the portrayed faces and bodies, Judith Elizabeth Weiss proposes a term of the "non-depicting portrait" whereby the presence of the portrayed subject "occurs under the condition of an inerasable difference between the seen and the imagined" (2013: 141).[1] Exploring the recent tendency within figurative art of such artists as David Hockney, Jacques Monory, and Mathilde Hiesse to account for the loss, absence, and disappearance of the human figure, Nancy argues that the function of what he calls the "other portrait" is no longer to reproduce a living person but instead to evoke its uncertain identity. Unlike the traditional portraiture that relies on mimetic representation of the sitter's unique subjectivity and whose aim is to render the subject's appearance, the "other portrait" proceeds from "an identity that is hardly supposed at all, but rather is evoked in its withdrawal" (2018: 94). The loss of self, the deformation of body, the withdrawal of subject—these are aesthetic modalities which any concept of the portrait should henceforth take into account.

But what happens when the disappearing subject is replaced by an object—does it become its mere substitute? And is there any chance this substitute could either make up for that loss of self or prevent the necessary reification of the represented and hence objectified subject? To answer these questions, this chapter will follow a figure of the empty chair which embodies, mediates, and materializes the absent subject across the literary, visual, theatrical, and sculptural works to argue for a seemingly paradoxical concept of the "portrait of absence." Based on the affective operation of shifting, and inspired by the recent nonmimetic approaches to the portrait, this concept embraces an aporetic bind between a mediation of the subject and its physical non-presence. Probing the formal work of the affects of loss, expectation, and desire, this chapter demonstrates how the empty chairs, grounded in the logic of disformation by shifting the subject into its invisibility, reinscribe the affective presence into the bodily absence to finally reconsider what the emptiness can really mean. Despite (or perhaps because of) the fact that in the history of portraiture, the chairs have had a purely practical reputation and mostly served as a mere device primarily designed to support the human body, both canonic and marginal artworks show otherwise: the chairs have been appearing with increasing frequency without humans to the point of a figural emancipation not only in the visual media but also in literature and on the stage.

Chairs without Sitters: Weiner, Kosuth, and the Missing Subject

Let us begin with the least known chair piece whose theoretical force is yet to be recognized beyond its Central European territory and which exceeds by far its usual modernist framing: a short story by Richard Weiner entitled "The Empty Chair" (Prázdná židle, 1916). Had there been a genre of "literary conceptualism," this radically innovative text whose main strategy is uncovered by its very subtitle "Analysis of an Unwritten Short Story," would arguably stand out as its referential point. Because Weiner's text is doing much more than is apparent at first glance; not only does it fake its own diegetic *failure*, a failure that is, in fact, a highly nuanced and dizzily intricate composition, but it also stages its main figure of the empty chair as a mediation of the absence that makes the subject present throughout its factual non-presence. The story of this "unwritten story" is seemingly simple: longing for solitude, a young man (Jan) living in Paris moves to a neighborhood where he knows no one. Several months later, he chances to meet his faithful friend (Václav) on the street; they are both very happy about the encounter and arrange an immediate visit. The friend is asked to bring a little refreshment from a nearby shop while the man hurries to his modest apartment to clean it up and make some tea. He puts two chairs and a table to the fireplace and waits. "He waits and waits. Moment after moment, hour after hour pass by and the prepared chair is still empty and waiting" (Weiner 1996: 380). The friend never comes, and the narrating protagonist is observing a "gaping" empty chair, brooding over why the longed-for visit turned into an even deeper and painful loneliness.

Yet the story is not what really matters here, or, at least, not from the point of view of the narrative voice which has an entirely different plan. For the explicit goal of the text is to explain, as precisely as possible, why the story has *never been written*. The real story behind that fictional anecdote is thus the story of a writing project that failed—a *failure of writing* that is nonetheless written about, commented upon, and described through and through exhaustively, as explained in the very first paragraph:

> The aim I have set myself in discussing the circumstances why this story was never actually written is senseless and is hardly excused

even if, as I believe, the following lines introduce an element of the fantastic, which would be far better used on some more suitable occasion, and of the eccentric, which would perhaps be more appropriate in a real story, whereas in the arguments presented here these will most likely serve only to lead the reader astray or to dead ends; there may also perhaps be found a degree of emotion or excitement (perhaps even agitation), which will most likely often confound my plan to present a pragmatic account of the demise of a literary work. (1996: 370)[2]

Right from the first sentence, Weiner's text takes up a peculiar discursive mode that one might call a "negative self-affirmation," that is, an antiphrasis which manifests and boasts a certain quality via its feigned negation. Such a strategy animates the Antic rhetorical figure of *meiosis*—widely used in the Renaissance poetry as a "*diminutio*" of a virtue and overlapping with the better known *litotes*, that is, the "understatement that intensifies" (Lanham 1991: 95)—which employs a "disabler" of an intentional weakening, underestimation, or euphemizing of a given elocution in order to reinforce its significance (Skinner 2007: 149). To put it otherwise, the text constitutes and affirms itself through its own self-negation. In fact, this mise en abyme play could be approached in the narratological terms as an asymmetry between the fictional discourse of the diegetic narrator rendering a virtual story and the metafictional discourse of the implied author, commenting on the failed short story. Analogously, the whole narrative conundrum could be summed up as a dominance of the metatextual *telling* over a textual *showing*, which is, after all, a recurrent pattern through which Weiner scholars read the piece.[3]

However, there is a catch with both readings applying rather uncritically the instruments from the narratological toolbox. For while the former fails to account for the fact that the "metafictional" voice of the implied author turns out to be the very "fictional" protagonist—at the moment of an inconspicuous switch of pronouns from the third person into "I"—the latter option overlooks Weiner's major strategy of *faking*: a discursive operation that blurs the boundaries between the diegetic and extra-diegetic levels on the way to a continual shifting between the absence and the presence of the story about an empty chair. The only scholar to notice both the affective and conceptual power of this contradiction is Peter Zusi, who in his brilliant analysis argues that "The Empty Chair" is basically a story of the double absence: while the first one operates at the level of the title referring to "the friend's uncanny absence and the man's uneasy solitude," the second involves "Weiner's textual failure: the absence of his story about absence" (2011: 136). As Zusi emphasizes, this "crucial parallel between the absent friend on the fictional level and the absent story on the meta-fictional level" demonstrates that *despite* what the text claims, the story is finally present: "This is the paradoxical conclusion of *The Empty Chair*, the story—the friend—arrives; the chair does not remain empty" (2011: 136n20, 142). The alleged narrative failure thus becomes a textual gain and the short-circuiting of the aesthetic forms generates a novel performative formation.

As if to alert the reader that a reliance on the message of the medium is not the right way to read it, the narrator's aim to discuss why the story has never been written is quickly rewritten as an intention not only to deal with a "horror that seized the host when the guest, whom he awaited and who promised that he would certainly come, did not show up" but also to "induce horror in the reader" (Weiner 1996: 378) through the lack of any rational explanation of the friend's failed visit. Disclosing this explicit affective strategy, Zusi underscores the performative charge of Weiner's metatext, which "is the enactment of that horror, for it acts out the compulsive generation of (unsatisfactory) explanations that is required to maintain the inexplicability that constitutes psychic horror" and due to which the whole text "does not depict a void; rather it fills a void through the compulsive proliferation of an explanatory structure" (Zusi 2011: 138, 139–140). While for Zusi, however, the pivotal textual strategy lies in the aforementioned shift among the narrating persons that "dispels the spectre of the metatext" (2011: 141), my argument holds that the crucial media-theoretical gesture of Weiner's text lies in the operative difference between the discursive and the performative, between what the text *says* and what it *does*. For when "The Empty Chair" presents a variety of the alternately suggested and immediately denied scenarios of how the story *could have*—if it would have had— taken place, coming up with several versions of what might have happened that the friend did not show up, it does nothing less than affirm that it *was* and *has been* "actually written."

And here lies the crux of the *negative self-affirmation* whereby the pretended handicap turns out to be a refined camouflage. The merely "intended," ceaselessly envisioned and allegedly failed story is here, taking place at the very moment of reading, through the generative emptiness of that horrifying chair. Speculating about the fictional mise-en-scène—or rather a *mise-en-chaise*—of his short story about an empty chair and planning its affective effects of excitement, agitation, and horror, the narrating protagonist is achieving the production of the story and triggering those affects right now. Emerging from the rift between utterance and performance, the conceptual gist of this "unwritten" short story consists in faking its failure while exposing, once again, the operative gap between what the text *says* about the narrative and its intended affective goals and what it, through this self-explanation, really *does*. And it is precisely this difference—a formal disharmony that turns the affect of horror into the object of speculation—that sustains the logic of the *diatext*, which, as the previous chapter argued, is a performative discourse grounded in the two-way mediality that merges the diegetic level of fiction with the autoreferential metatext, a media operation that performs the affective work of forms *through* disclosing their structure.

But how, one could rightly wonder, does such a reading keep the pace with the mediaphilosophical premise of paying attention not only to the theoretical qualities of each medium but also to the material basis of their mediality? In order not to remain baffled in front of the mute chair, endlessly interrogating its intricate and encoded meanings—which is the project of hermeneutics that can easily alter to the proverbial Gestalt therapy method of the so-called "*Leerer-Stuhl-Technik*" (empty chair technique) in which feelings and hidden assumptions are exchanged between a real person and the imagined "other" sitting on a chair—we should now turn to the object around which Weiner's text is structured, since we barely scratched the surface of it so far. And yet it is this piece of furniture that generates the emptiness both *on* the diegetic chair and *within* the text as a trace of the subject that never came, as a trace of absence inscribing the lack into the performative discourse. To probe the performative mechanisms and affective force of this emptiness further, it seems necessary to consider other chairs made both before and after Weiner's short story.

The specific mediality of Weiner's empty chair, drawing on the oscillation between *doing* and *telling*, blurring the clear-cut distinctions between presence and absence, and sustaining the speculative force of the "diatext," finds its echo in one of the founding works of conceptual art, Joseph Kosuth's *One and Three Chairs* (1965; Figure 4.1). Kosuth's triple artwork contains an object in the shape of a wooden folding chair, its mounted full-scale photograph hung on the wall on its left, and photographic enlargement of the short text offering a lexical definition of the word "chair" which is placed on the gallery wall on the right side from the "real" wooden chair. Demonstrating a single chair in three different forms—as a material artefact (object), as a photographic reproduction (image), as a dictionary entry (text)—this gallery installation stages not only an arbitrary but also a conflicting

Figure 4.1 Joseph Kosuth, *One and Three Chairs*, 1965. Museum of Modern Art (MoMA), New York. Wikimedia Commons.

relationship between signifier and signified. As a result, the threefold chair both announces and performs a claim that the same chair can never be identical when rendered by different media forms.

At the same time, however, this intermedia configuration brings to the fore a latency of specific forms to open up their different versions and deployments; the latency that is underlaid by a mute work of the absence that gives the triple chair both its performative and affective forces. As for its verbal construction, Kosuth's multiplied—and one might say *multi-folded* as it repeatedly unfolds and refolds its own discursive and material forms—chairs show, as pointed out by Cary Wolfe, that "language is just as important by what it does *not* communicate as by what it does communicate" (2010: 242). Arising from a rift between the present representations, concepts, and material things as well as from the uncanny horizontal composition through which they reject any idea of a chair's practical purpose of sitting, this *non-communication* aspect is key. It constitutes a generative disturbance to the formal whole that collapses upon the encounter with a potential sitter who is forced to shift not only between the chair's different mediations but also among the sitter's positions. Such is the affective operation of shifting triggered by these empty chairs, a shifting that moves in two ways as it relates both to the—missing, coming, and leaving—subject and to the forms that continually switch between their different mediations. We can thus push one step further Belting's claim that Kosuth's artwork is based on a tricky juxtaposition of picture and description, "wiping out the traditional distinctions: the picture here is also reduced to mere definition. Seen as a whole, the commentary triumphs over the work, which it causes to disappear" (2003: 20), to argue that the indispensable part of this juxtaposition is the *subject, present in its absence*. Through its tangible lack and non-presence this missing subject, be it a spectator or a virtual sitter, becomes the fourth element of Kosuth's installation, a medium of its performative and affective force.

The operational inversion that Weiner plays out in his short story is hence taken up by Kosuth in his dismantling the traditional distinction between a commentary and a commented object, between showing and telling, which ultimately replaces these boundaries by a performative diatext. But although both of them transform an ordinary empty chair into the speculative object of an endless interrogation that replies with a proliferation of an unsatisfactory self-referential commentary, through a lack of the subject, and by a mute multiplication, it is Kosuth's immobile yet disconcerting triple "apparatus" that does—paradoxically enough being not a purely discursive object—unfold the theoretical work of shifting further. Specifically, the multiplication of the chair and its various mediations puts on head the structuralist founding claim about the necessary *erasure* of a real thing once this thing is named. So when Lacan in 1966, roughly at the same time when Kosuth' piece was exhibited, proposed that the linguistic prerequisite consists in the fact that the word is always already "a presence made of absence" and that "from this articulated couple of presence and absence [. . .] a language's world of meaning is born, in which the world of things will situate itself" (2006a: 228), *One and Three Chairs* radically questions this linguistic *a priori* by simply staging this absence inherent to the discursive presence right next to the referent's material presence. This absence is shifted and ultimately short-circuited by another absence, the absence of the subject.

Tracing the Present Absence with van Gogh, Derrida, and Nancy

When the author of "The Empty Chair" was four years old, a small town in southern France saw one of the most dramatic events in the history of the nineteenth-century painting. After many months of waiting, filled with dozens of letters full of expectations sent to his longed-for friend, on October 23, 1888, Paul Gauguin finally arrived in Arles to stay with Vincent van Gogh in the Yellow House. However, as described in Gauguin's memoirs *Avant et après* (Before and After, 1903) and his rich correspondence, the much-awaited creative atmosphere in their new home quickly turned into a high-strung place full of angry discord and quarrels. During the months of November and December, their frequent arguments escalated, accompanied by the tormenting southern mistral and constant sleets. After one of these dramatic disputes, Gauguin went for an evening walk and suddenly heard steps behind him. He looked back and saw Vincent rushing at him with an open razor in his hand. When Gauguin boldly stepped in his direction, Vincent turned away and ran back. That night, Gauguin decided to rather stay at a nearby hotel, while Vincent ran home and, seized by the visual and auditory hallucinations, has cut a piece of his ear, wrapped it up in a sheet of paper and delivered this piece of his own flesh to his favorite prostitute Rachel—as "a gesture reminiscent of the matador who awards the ear of the bull he has killed to a favored lady" (Maurer 1998: 81).

The legendary story about a conflict between two irreconcilable artists would be of no interest here unless it provides a multifarious affective impulse that would have been shaping van Gogh's work—an affective trigger of solitude, loss, and desire that would be made explicit and would drive the forms of another chair composition. For the present argument, in other words, the *bio-graphical* account is relevant only insofar as it makes the "bio" a subsequent result of the *graphein* that *writes* one's life and whose visible traces are *inscribed* into van Gogh's canvas which then becomes, to paraphrase Derrida, the "biothanato-graphic" scene of writing (1987: 336). Resuming that anecdote, van Gogh's biographers rightly ask: "Why did van Gogh, who so relished the encounter of painter and sitter, not do a portrait of Gauguin?" (Metzger and Walter 1997: 458).[4] The paradox of the absence of a portrait hence culminates within the violent quarrel from which emerge two 1888 paintings of empty and yet occupied chairs: *Vincent's Chair with his Pipe* and *Gauguin's Chair* (Figures 4.2; 4.3).

Instead of a serene still life, which their silent objecthood could suggest, the diptych of these lonely symbol-laden chairs constitute a fairly disharmonic and radically desubjectifying portraits of absence. On the one hand, both chairs that differ from each other in their colors, composition, atmosphere, thickness of impasto, and style make an organic part of van Gogh's repertoire of the material imagery imbuing

Disformations

Figure 4.2 Vincent van Gogh, *La Chaise de Vincent*, 1888. National Gallery, London. Wikimedia Commons.

the most ordinary things with a force of life and symbolism. On the other hand, their symbolic role gives way to a non-allegorical *mediality* which replaces the presence of the—living but leaving—subject with an empty space that plays the role of its *substitute*. While *Vincent's Chair* operates at once as a metonymic self-portrait and a portrait of affects that are yet to come, *Gauguin's Chair* stands for a metonymic portrait of the hitherto present but already disappearing friend—a chair that is no longer occupied by van Gogh's irritable friend Paul but rather by his arriving loyal companion: a specter of loneliness.[5]

Although these substitutes certainly provoke the feelings of solitude, pain, loss, and void one should not rush to enclose their formal dynamic within the bounds of *the work of mourning* which, according to Freud, makes one to overcome a painful fact "that the loved object no longer exists" (1981: 244). It is most likely that the *Trauerarbeit* lies at the origin of the diptych but especially Gauguin's empty chair does much to counter the soothing and transformative process of mourning. Rather

Figure 4.3 Vincent van Gogh, *Le Fauteuil de Gauguin*, 1888. Van Gogh Museum, Amsterdam. Wikimedia Commons.

than providing a cure, a relief, a promise of replacing the absence by other's presence, it relentlessly revolves around the loss, asserts the empty space, and reinvigorates the lack by means of surrogating the other for a few objects recalling the absent person. If there is mourning on the pictorial level of showing and telling—for "[t]he object has not perhaps actually died, but has been lost as an object of love" (Freud 1981: 245)—there is also its opposite on the performative level of the painting's doing. By staging and, indeed, thickening the traces of the subject's absence through the commemorative objects including a lit candle and two solid books that irreducibly underscore the sitter's not being here, *Gauguin's Chair* insists on the *irreplaceability* of the subject, making this portrait of absence endlessly reiterate the lack and desire. Less than a pure work of mourning, the performative capacity of this affective object thus comes closer to what Margaret Iversen (in a different context of the war memorials) phrases as an "antithesis to mourning," or the "anti-mourning": a failed *Trauerarbeit* that "instead of undoing affective attachments [...] establishes a cathexis by reopening an archaic psychic wound" (2007: 105). This reopening of a wound that constantly accentuates the lack through a reification of the empty space which, in turn, extends and reformulates the very missing subject stands for a circular affective process that one might also call a "counter-mourning."

The empty chairs should not be read either solely as manifestations of melancholia that Freud describes as a pathological stage of mourning that "behaves like an open wound, drawing to itself cathectic energies [. . .] from all directions and emptying the ego until it is totally impoverished" and which is based on an "*identification* of the ego with the abandoned object" (1981: 249, 253). Rather than establishing such an identification and being interiorized by and in the subject, the loss and the lack are *exteriorized* by placing the empty space, left after the subject, on the chair. The portrait of absence thus also operates as a portrait of *desire* in that it is "indissolubly bound to 'mnesic trace'" (Laplanche and Pontalis 1988: 482) around which the chair revolves— desire which is at once driven by the lack but also disturbed by the memory of the *failed encounter*, a long-awaited encounter that went all wrong and shifted the sitter in flesh into the empty space.[6]

Such desire has its specific spatial arrangement that ejects the subject toward the object of its desire. Despite the seemingly domestic atmosphere surrounding both chairs with a shade of familiarity, the paintings' *mise-en-chaise*—by which I mean the entire scene that is structured not only from the point of view of a spectator but also as the affective site focalized from the position of the chair—does not allow a calm contemplation but rather gives shape to a kind of tense expectation. Barely silent companions that would allow to overcome the loss, both chairs are situated and placed into a confronting position, a formation that comes about through a disconcerting perspective of the gaze seized by vertigo. Both the material attributes and perspective thus convey a raw message: while the chair is and will be here, the subject has left and will never come again.

But has the subject that had gone really vanished? Hardly so, because what van Gogh's painting shows is that the missing subject has imprinted its absence into the form of a stubbornly present affective trace. "While the trace is visible, what produces it remains withdrawn and invisible," notices Sybille Krämer in her account on temporality of the trace to further argue that such a trace "visualize[s] the non-presence of what is left behind. The trace embodies not the absent thing itself, but rather its absence" (2015: 174). Despite—and because of—the absence of the subject, van Gogh's empty chair constitutes an affectively and semiotically overdetermined object for as a *metaphor*, it symbolizes the material force of things living their own "withdrawn" lives; as an *index*, it refers to the ongoing "bio-graphical" conflict and the disappearing subject who is just about to leave the scene; and as a *trace*, it gives shape to the pain, loss, lack, and desire while making present the absence of the subject. The desire shaped by the object of the empty chair is then not so much, as Lacan holds, "mediated by reference to Nothingness" for "the true object-cause of desire [. . .] is, by definition, a 'metonymy of lack'" (Žižek 2000: 107) but rather oriented to an *elsewhere* of the lost subject, the subject that emerges through a disturbing present trace on the portrait.

But since the subject—as the main object of any portrait—is gone, is it then appropriate to still talk about the portrait? In order to make this point clearer, let us now take a closer look at how Nancy elaborates the notion of portrait in his recent works dealing with this manifold genre in both classical and contemporary visual arts. Exploring the position and structure of the subject in relation to the look that constitutes the central problem of portraiture, Nancy, in his 2000 essay *Le Regard du portrait* (The Look of the Portrait), observes a situation of the modernist subject which is no longer "the self-evidence of an interiority held within itself by the suspension of the world," since this subject threw off "resemblance and recollection understood in terms of humanism, intentionality, and representation" (2018: 40–41). In his later book *L'Autre Portrait* (published in English as "The Other Portrait" together with the former essay), Nancy fleshes out the oft-dismissed and yet crucial etymology of the French verb *portraire*, a composite of the prefix *por-* (for) and the verb *traire* (to draw, e.g., a line). Within the regime of figuration and representation, "the prefix *por* (originally *pour*) marks an intensification: the line, the outline is applied or carried forth and its intensity sends it in the direction of a substitution of the drawing of the thing drawn" (2018: 47).

The gesture of *substitution*—a visual stroke, or a line, surrogating a singular *trait* and hence putting one trace in place of another—that activates the *supplementary* operation of replacing a preexisting subject while adding a new one, is therefore an always already present condition of the genre of portraiture, no matter to which artistic media those mimetic lines that outline a new figure belong to. If the supplement, as Derrida argues, comprises two mutually opposed yet complementary meanings of an addition, "a surplus, a plenitude enriching another plenitude" and a substitute which fills a void, "adds only to replace" and whose "place is assigned in the structure by the mark of an emptiness" (2016: 157), the portrait fundamentally and always follows the logic of supplement.

Taking Nancy's etymological insight one step further, it would not be difficult to see how the supplementary logic of portraiture involves another Derrida's concept, the one of "differance." As the *OED* tells us, the word "portrait" comes from the Latin *protrahere,* meaning "to draw forward," "to reveal," "to extend," "to prolong," or "to defer" (*OED,* s.v. "portrait"). Along with the act of substitution, this Derridean inflection would thus also allow to understand the portrait as a media operation that at once *reveals* and *suspends* the subject. But Nancy has more to say about the concept whose investment in the logic of representation should not be taken for granted. Observing the tendency within contemporary figurative art to account for the loss, absence, and disappearance of the human figure, he applies a fitting notion of the "other portrait," the function of which is no longer to reproduce a living person but instead to *evoke* its distanced and uncertain identity. Unlike the traditional portrait that "proceeds from a presupposed identity, one whose appearance must be rendered," the latter "proceeds from an identity that is hardly supposed at all, but rather is evoked in its withdrawal" (2018: 94). This founding moment of withdrawal takes us back, once again, to the genre's etymological affluence for, as Nancy emphasizes, in its Italian designation, *il ritratto* signifies not only portraiture but also retreat, retraction, and *withdrawal.* Since the relationship between the portrayal and the person portrayed cannot be accounted for within the regime of identity, representation, and reproduction, what comes to the fore in the portrait is always "the other" who "withdraws in showing itself; it makes a retreat within its very expression" (2018: 49). This other is hence not a new ontological entity, but the one who comes up in the dynamic of a present absence, emerging in absentia, and disappearing while appearing.

On the portrait of absence, the subject is removed, replaced, and literally *unseated*, while the trace of an absence takes its place. And this is a major paradox of this portrait because through its very physical absence, the missing subject is enacted not only as a present formation but also as an amplified one. Van Gogh and Weiner thus make a double gesture: they intensify the presence of the subject by its physical absence while saving the subject—by its very (non)depiction—from the status of a mere object, from its reification. The double temporality of the empty chairs thus informs a portrait that is brought not *ad absurdum* but rather *ad fontes* and also *ex post*. Returning before the arrival of the subject, before its physical presence and firmly situated position, the portrait of absence, at the same time, prefigures and outlines its departure, loss, and lack. Such a portrait shifts the negativity of an absent or disappearing subject into a generative lack, a lack that stages the presence of the missing subject via its tangible absence.

Chairing Not Sharing, Shifting Not Sitting: A Media Swap in Ionesco's The Chairs

To be sure, there are a considerable number of other empty chairs that have emerged between modernism and now that do display either a classical figure of mourning or a monument of the "counter-mourning." The former is provided by, for instance, Egon Schiele's expressionist poster for the 1918 exhibition of the Vienna Secession (*Secession 49. Ausstellung*) made shortly after the death of Gustav Klimt, wherein an empty chair in the foreground of the angular table surrounded by sitting readers stands for a visual epitaph for the deceased artist. Prominently, the latter can be seen in the work of Doris Salcedo who, at the occasion of the Eighth International Istanbul Biennial in 2013, managed to jam 1550 wooden chairs between two crumbling buildings in a city's working-class neighborhood as a memorial to what the sculptor calls a general "topography of war."[7] What makes, however, the chair disformations by Weiner and van Gogh different from those memorial sites is not only the supplementary structure of their central objects but also the affective work of shifting between the lack of a missing subject *qua* its absent presence and the unfulfilled promise of its arrival—a swap grounded in the collision between what the empty chairs show and what they do. In his beautiful essay on the chair-monuments whose affective force lies in their capacity to merge the past and the future, Pietro Conte addresses this double temporality by arguing that "the pathos of an empty chair relates both to the memory of loss and the announcement of a return or of a new arrival" (2013: 127–28). And it is precisely this announcement of someone who could, should, and is desired to come—if only something didn't go wrong—that sustains the emptiness replacing the subject for good. But while the chair anatomy may well recall a sitting human shape, once these four-legged objects multiply, their unsettling capacity to dispose of the subject becomes even stronger.[8]

Taking the aesthetics of the empty chairs' generative disturbances and their mediality of the absent subject onto the theatrical stage,

Ionesco's play *The Chairs: A Tragic Farce* (1952) gives their portrait modality another spin through their accumulation that transforms a quiet piece of furniture into a site of the restless and self-devouring waiting. The *Chairs*' plot follows two main protagonists in their nineties who go by the names of Old Man and Old Woman as they frantically run across the stage, preparing chairs for invisible guests who are expected to come in order to listen to the Old Man's revelatory message which is supposed to disclose to the audience a great mystery of life but which needs to be delivered only by an Orator. After the suicide of both protagonists, however, it becomes clear that the long-awaited messenger is a deaf-mute. As the chairs accumulate and multiply, gradually piling up to all sides of the stage, communication as well as performance of both protagonists fall apart. While in the first scenes of the play, the pretended presence of the invisible guests is mimetically performed via the illustrative actions and gestures of the two hosts, constantly moving and shifting the empty chairs, later on—throughout the catastrophe and a somewhat failed catharsis— the accumulation of the chair-guests reaches a point when the present absence can only be articulated through a performative language that takes up the formal and affective work of the empty chairs.

In order to shed some light on the performative bind between the emptiness and the discursive work of the chairs, it is important to look more closely on the way the ambivalent absence is staged. At first, the present chairs play the role of a pure substitute whose main function is to evoke the gradually increasing invisible guests; an illusion that is, nonetheless, undermined by an unsettling tension between those who are visible and those who are not. By emphasizing the impossibility of this illusion—precisely in the manner of Barthesian self-disclosing "*Larvatus prodeo*"[9]—*The Chairs* rephrase the foundational fictional pact of "suspension of disbelief" into a suspecting formula calling for a "sustaining of disbelief":

[*The Old Man and Old Woman re-enter together, leaving space between them for their guest. She is invisible.*]
OLD MAN: [*to the Lady*]: Let me get you a chair. [. . .]
   [*The Old Man and Old Woman smile. They even laugh. They appear to be very amused by the story the invisible Lady tells them. A pause, a moment of silence in the conversation. Their faces lose all expression.*]
   [. . .]
[*Some embarrassing things take place, invisibly.*] (1958: 123, 128)

As the chairs accumulate on the stage, so does the absence faced by the protagonists and spectators. Intensified by the hosts' frequent ramming into the piled chairs with which, at the same time, they struggle to communicate, this absence gains tangible and oppressive forms. The key role of both the emptiness and absence in *The Chairs* did not obviously go unnoticed by Ionesco scholars. "The absence of identity is thus literally materialized," notes Thomas Edeling aptly and he further argues that "the weight of the protagonists in a metaphorical sense is substituted by a counterweight materialized by the objects" (2009: 36). As was the case with Weiner and van Gogh, Ionesco's play rethinks the absence as a paradoxical mode of presence that is driven by the affects of lack, loss, and desire rather than as a pure non-presence.

No matter how a particular performance of *The Chairs* stresses it, Ionesco's stage direction leaves no doubt about the dialectic nature of this absence that emerges from the firm link between emptiness and accumulation: "*There must be very many chairs on the stage: at least forty, even more if possible. They are accumulating very quickly, ever quicker. It is an accumulation. The stage is buried under these chairs,* that crowd of present absences [la foule des *absences présentes*]" (1991: 167; emphasis added).[10] Although the denouement of the play, during which spectators are left with the heaps of empty chairs littered with confetti, might imply that this emptiness is a consequence of the overall dramatic fiasco—the awaited orator is deaf-mute, the two main protagonists kill themselves, the longed-for celebration is ruined, and the central message has not been delivered—the chair formations do not leave us with a nothingness of the void but rather with an "emptiness that is not completely *empty*" (Edeling 2009: 43).[11] Rather than embodying a negative ontological *stasis*, this emptiness operates as a performative disturbance constantly shifting between the presence and the absence—as such, it cannot be complete for it is constantly disrupted by the presence of the missing subjects, by "that crowd of present absences" which fills the void of the empty chairs and makes them the main protagonists. Such is also an irony of the final sonic shift when the indistinct human voices come from under the piled empty chairs and transform the seeming void into a loud absence. After all, the guests did arrive for the hosts have brought them in themselves.

Overfilling the space of the stage into all directions and even heaping up onto one another, the chairs' substitutional role becomes voided insofar as the invisibility of the guests evolves into an impossibility of their presence. The empty chair as a *substitute* thus quickly turns into the *supplement* that does not merely take place of a missing subject but also adds itself to the present void on the stage; it stands irrefutably here in its materiality while blocking the view of the protagonists and thwarting any attempt of a symbolical interpretation. Hence, when the "*Old Woman puts the chair behind the four others, then exits by door No.8 and re-enters by door No.5, after a few moments, with another chair that she places beside the one she has just brought in*" (1958: 130), what is repeatedly moved and removed is not a metaphysical index of the absence, nor an autonomous "withdrawn" object but rather a chair that both replaces and disturbs.

What both Ionesco's stage directions and the actual performance of the protagonists unfold no more as an invisibility of the guests but as their far more vexing absence—the absence that is performed rather than named by the whole *mise-en-chaise* of the play—is dramatically at odds with the language whose task is nothing less than to create (an illusion of) the invisible presence while uncovering it as an absence.[12] On the one hand, the language gives names to the "invisible" phantomlike guests and therefore literally seats them on the empty chairs. On the other, and more importantly, the dialogues of the protagonists absorb the emptiness of the chairs themselves: not only the awkward movements of jolting the chairs along the stage but also their loud rattling. The latter is, in turn, taken up by the disjointed rhythm of the protagonists' lines as well as unfolded through the hasty juxtaposition of the subjects and objects, resulting into a clash that ultimately expels anyone's symbolical presence.

> OLD MAN: Sit down, sit down, the ladies with the ladies, and the
> gentlemen with the gentlemen, or vice versa, if you prefer . . . We
> don't have any more nice chairs . . . we have to make do with what
> we have . . . I'm sorry . . . take the one in the middle . . . does anyone
> need a fountain pen? [. . .]
> OLD MAN: my wife . . . Mr. . . . Mrs. . . . my wife . . . Mr. . . . Mrs. . . . my
> wife . . .
> OLD WOMAN: Who are all these people, my darling? [. . .]
> OLD MAN: More people! More chairs! More people! More chairs!
> Come in, come in, ladies and gentlemen . . . Semiramis, faster . . .
> We'll give you a hand soon! (1958: 138, 143)

Importantly, the accumulative chair formations trigger the affects of expectation, confusion, and frustration—bound to the missing subject— but also the affective operation of shifting that rewrites the subject through the chairs' constant displacement and by situating the subject between presence and absence, visibility and invisibility, a human thing and, indeed, a wooden thing. Since its paradoxical mediality is poised between the missing subject that it substitutes and the object whose main role is to emphasize the absence, the empty chair operates as both a specific piece of furniture and a *shifter*, that is, an empty signifier whose main function is not to signify but to designate (Lacan 2006b: 677). The chair that *at once is and is not* a chair was precisely a concern that puzzled Wittgenstein in his *Philosophical Investigations* (1953) that was published posthumously only one year after Ionesco's piece.

> I say, "There is a chair over there." What if I go to fetch it, and it suddenly disappears from sight?—"So it wasn't a chair, but some kind of illusion."—But a few seconds later, we see it again and are able to touch it, and so on.—"So the chair was there after all, and its disappearance was some kind of illusion."—But suppose that after a time it disappears again—or seems to disappear. What are we to say now? Have you rules ready for such cases—rules saying *whether such a thing is still to be called a "chair"*? But do we miss them when we use the word "chair"? And are we to say that we do not really attach any meaning to this word, because we are not equipped with rules for every possible application of it? (Wittgenstein 2009: 42; emphasis added)

Read in line with the present argument about the generative work of disformations, this short paragraph demonstrates how a tangible emptiness of a chair has a capacity to explode the semantic integrity of language. For "whether such a thing is still to be called a 'chair'" is not only a question addressed by philosophy of language but, once we add the adjective *empty*, it also becomes a vexing question posed to form by the paradoxical portrait of absence. Of course, while in the case of van Gogh's, Weiner's, and Ionesco's chairs, the tension between the presence and absence is generated through the combination of the supplementary logic, lack, expectation, and desire, Wittgenstein is not concerned with a chair lacking its human counterpart but rather with a chair that simply ceases to be one. But are their concerns really so different? While Wittgenstein explores a situation of dispersion of the referent itself, or, more precisely, disappearing of all its forms and mediations for which language has no capacity to designate, he also asks a question which is of an utmost relevance for the performative mediality of Ionesco's *The Chairs*: Has a word any significance at all when it cannot name a form that finds itself in a paradoxical situation? And is a chair still the object *as* language signifies it, once it radically changes its actions?

One would rather expect, and rightly so, such a Wittgensteinian inflection in the first part of this chapter dealing with Kosuth's installation. Indeed, the impact of Wittgenstein's thought on the conceptual art hardly needs restating and Kosuth himself made this influence explicit in his essay "Art after Philosophy" (1969) when paraphrasing the philosopher's famous formula that "the meaning is the use" (1991: 15), which moves the problem of meaning from referentialism to the domain of pragmatic situation. What I want to argue, however, is that the highly confusing *shifting* of Wittgenstein's chair that respectively appears and disappears, signifies and dismantles the signification, is undertaken by Ionesco who transforms the formal work of shifting into the affective operation that is triggered by the chairs' accumulation and that, in turn, rewrites the absence of the subject into its bewildering presence. While Wittgenstein puts in play the possibility of a hyper-semanticized language that would be equipped "for every possible application of it," including the one of the parallel existence and non-existence, Ionesco's play expands this potential through the supplementary structure of the empty chairs whose aim is no more to be seated by the subjects but to change position with them.

Decentered, Not Vanished

In place of a conclusion, there is one more empty chair, a giant wooden chair that rises 7.5 meters high, weighs around 20 tons, and stands right next to the entrance to the Weimar University Library (Figure 4.4). Made by the sculptor Hermann Bigelmayr, its title *Lehrstuhl – leerer Stuhl* (Chair—Empty Chair, 2005) may well be a pun that, as the artist's web portfolio explains, plays with a double meaning of the word *Stuhl*—involving, on the one hand, a reference to a scholarly position of the "academic chair" and, on the other, a simple empty seat expected to be taken by a reader or a student—but its position, posture, and materiality do outwit the wit of the title. There is an anthrodecentric stance in Bigelmayr's sculpture not so much bound to its size that can easily evoke an inhuman giant who could smash the whole library into pieces with a single wave of its hand.

What the gargantuan oak construction incorporates is rather a shift from any humanist idea of an autonomous and self-contained subject to the subject as a medium operating between other subjects and objects, a shift that "reveal[s] the extent to which the human actor has always already been decentred *by* the technical object" (Siegert 2015: 193).[13]

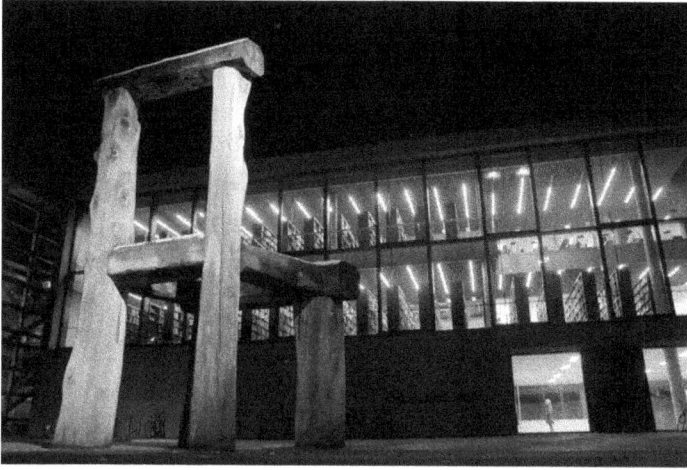

Figure 4.4 Hermann Bigelmayr, *Lehrstuhl—leerer Stuhl* (2005). Bauhaus-Universität, Weimar. Wikimedia Commons.

Instead of symbolizing a lack, the affective force of the chair's crowded emptiness lies in the simple act of substitution, a swap of one subject for another. Reading Bigelmay's chair in its spatial coordinates, as it rises above the hustle and bustle of the passing readers, it stands for a mediaphilosophical object par excellence for it allows "to view the human as a link in a connection that encompasses both nature and culture and is virtually inconceivable without transmission" (Krämer 2015: 220). Different people will come and leave, conveying their mundane messages, but the chair will remain here, through its empty seat ceaselessly questioning not only those messages but also the alleged irreplaceability of their messengers.

The empty chairs by Weiner, van Gogh, and Ionesco constitute a paradoxical *portrait of absence* that makes the subject present through its physical non-presence. These seemingly mute and passive objects have a capacity not only to dispose of but also to replace the subject with a disturbing—for incomplete—emptiness, an emptiness that makes the subject present through a swap of the missing subject for its present affective trace. Staging an absence of the subject while provoking desire for its presence—such is the core of the affective operation of shifting that the empty chairs trigger when they ultimately decenter the subject. That the subject is decentered does not, though, imply that it becomes deactivated. On the contrary, the empty chairs that operate in the visual, literary, and theatrical forms show clearly that as long as the subjects remain in the paradoxical situation of the present absence, their field of action remains richer than in a state of a sheer presence. And if their physical absence intensifies their affective presence, it also means that the subject, no matter how invisible or non-present, can never really vanish. In the end, then, one might wonder if there is such a thing as an empty chair at all.

CODA

AFFECTIVE COMPOUNDS MAKE A MEDIA EXCESS

Each figure explodes, vibrates in and of itself like a sound severed from any tune—or is repeated to satiety, like the motif of a hovering music.

Roland Barthes, *A Lover's Discourse: Fragments*, 1977

If the major claim of this book was that formal dissonances, distortions, and disturbances are driven by specific affective operations that push the recognizable forms to the limits of representation, with the overall argument that through linking the disturbances to form with the affective agency can we learn something new about the aesthetic and theoretical force of media, then what remains is to add a few words on the inextricable entanglement between the formal work of affects and the affective work of media. Only scarcely have cultural affect theory and media philosophy engaged in a vigorous dialogue, oddly enough given the attention that many affect theorists pay to the operational qualities of affects and their relational frameworks which are possible only due to their two-way mediality between the force of *affectus* and the effects of *affectio* that Brinkema phrases as "the double bind of affect" (2014: 24). And yet these affective frameworks arise from specific mediations between various networks, situations, and cultural objects that are inseparable from the concrete media that allow them.

The same conceptual flaw can be detected in the broadly construed scholarly field of media philosophy that, despite its emphasis on the material basis of the artistic media and its theoretical inquiry into ways media perform their own reflection, tends to dismiss—with a few important exceptions including the works of Mark Hansen (2003), Steven Shaviro (2010), Christiane Voss (2019), or Bernd Herzogenrath (2019)—the formal and intermedia agency of affects altogether, despite the fact that a large number of those scholars build upon Bergson's key notion "that there is no perception without affection" (1991: 58). Rather than filling this gap, in what follows I simply want to propose that opening a dialogue between the fields of affect theory and media philosophy is necessary not only for a better understanding of their objects but also in order to unpack what seems to be a direct link between an affective interaction and what I would like to call a media excess.

One of the main tasks of the previous close readings of various encounters with the generative disturbances to form was to demonstrate that if an analysis of the affective agency of forms is to have any conceptual payoff at all, it is vital to undertake such an analysis beyond the scope of isolated artworks and investigate that agency, instead, in its figural movement across different media and contexts. To this aim, the present strategy of thinking through and with the intermedia figures in their aesthetic rearrangements and transhistorical movement across literary, visual, and audiovisual media was employed and it showed these figures as both aesthetically and theoretically rich sites of disformations that interconnect the affective work of forms with the formal work of affects. Hence, while the figure of the *faceless face* interconnects modernist aesthetics of the formless with the historical experience of the real across literary texts and images, the *wallpaper pattern* compels us to think the picturesque rococo engravings together with a cinematic 1961 family drama and with a piece of contemporary video art. Subsequently, the figure of the *garbage dump* accounted for the epistemological potential of rubbish not only in a French postmodern novel but also in a garbology research undertaken in the North American city of Tucson, through a totalitarian motif of typewriters discarded at a scrap heap in Stalinist Czechoslovakia, and against the backdrop of a dump in New York City. The figure of the *empty chair*, then, staged an intermedia encounter among two post-impressionist canvases from the end of the nineteenth century, a Central European modernist short story from 1916, a canonic installation of 1960s conceptual art, and a contemporary sculpture made of wood in 2005. Instead of media and contextual specificity, these intermedia figures are grounded in the travels, survivals, and latent dialogues between disparate poetics, historical framings, and cultural boundaries.

That the artworks think not so much by conveying propositional statements—that is, what their images, texts, and sounds intentionally represent and express—but rather through their performative mechanisms, speculative gestures, and affective operations, was the other premise of this book. If the mediaphilosophical perspective holds that media reveal "an oscillation and communication between informed matter and materialized information" and in so doing they "come to matter as the mediality of reflection" (Herzogenrath 2015: 5, 7), the proposed concept of *disformations*, based on the dialectic of form and deformation, which permanently puts in question what form actually *is* and *does*, how it thinks with various artworks, and how it can actually be thought across different media, thus comes about as a mediaphilosophical concept in its own right. Furthermore, by unpacking how the aesthetic forms trigger new figural thought across various sites of disformations, the preceding chapters have invited us to rethink the borderlands between the discursive and the nondiscursive. This is also a sound reason why, I would wager, media philosophy should share its usual investment in the art of moving image, film, and photography with literature that has a powerful potential of what Tom Eyers recently called "speculative formalism," not least because the latter stages "the manner in which, far from shutting down the possibility of meaning, the impossibility of any final, formal integration of a structure and its components parts is the very condition of possibility of that structure" (2017: 8). Rather than being a firmly established logocentric institution, literature, to put it once more with Malabou, stands for the *plastic* work of writing and as such, it permanently opens, undoes, and reforms the form en route to stage an encounter of the discursive with the visual while putting into play the sonic and brushing the haptic.

While what this book argued for as disformations can be understood as an excessive, decentering, and overdetermined movement of forms driven by specific affective operations that rewrite form and push it to novel formations, this movement has crucial consequences for the mediality of these new forms in motion. Indebted to van Alphen's assertion that "the affective operations and the way they shock to thought are what opens a space for the not yet known" (2008: 30), the endeavor of my analyses was to offer both specific and generalizable operations of shattering, saturating, evaluating, and shifting which, on the one hand, engage in the desubjectifying force of affects and, on the other, release the affects' performative qualities. The performativity of affects, I have claimed, emerges from within an incessant work of forms and takes its shape in the intermedia figures.

What could remain rather implicit throughout those analyses, however, is the fact that each of the affective operations always involves several mutually interacting affects rather than a single, let alone a pure, one. In case of the faceless face, the affective operation of *shattering* was grounded in the combination of horror, shock, and disgust, but also fascination. The *saturating*, then, enacted by the excessive details of the wallpaper ornaments, was built upon the affect of fascination as well but was possible only due to its further entanglement with fear, confusion, and boredom.

What allowed the affective operation of *revaluating* of the garbage dump and reconfigured it as a powerful speculative object was the mixture of obsession, curiosity, desire, and disgust. Finally, the affective operation of *shifting*, structured around the figure of the empty chair, was driven by the functional coalescence of loss, expectation, irony, and desire.

By no means should this observation reject a possible circulation of a singular affect engendered by given situation or formal arrangement and enticing a specific feeling or emotion; what I simply argue is that the stronger the affective agency of the aesthetic forms is, the more the specific affects tend to accumulate into what could be dubbed "affective compounds." Without any doubt, distinct affects can still be distinguished within these affective compounds but their performative force—that is, what these affects do, how and to what extent they operate within and upon form—results precisely from their *interaction* and therefore entails more than a mere sum of their parts. The very close readings of various disturbances to form then provide a useful approach to how these affective interactions can be detected, analyzed, and thought. What I therefore want to argue is that this affective accumulation and, indeed, overdetermination lead to a peculiar *media excess*. For in the moments that are oversaturated with the agency of different affects, the generic boundaries between various media modalities of the discursive, the visual, and the sonic collide and blur. The sites of disformations, read across the four intermedia figures, made the case of the two-way excess of affects and media, one that mutually transforms each other.

To give just two examples of this affective-media excess: when the faceless face ceased to be a mere shocking image, firmly rooted in the repertoire of cinematic and literary imagination, and became also an object of fascination, fear, and horror that structured the rhythm of language while shaping the disruptive mute scream, its visual force contributed to its discursive and sonic qualities which altogether—disturbingly yet generatively—corrupted and shattered the formal integrity of the face. While the empty chair, then, on the journey of a gradual displacing of the subject might at first appear as a symbol of loss and mourning, once its shifting forms triggered the other affects of expectation, confusion, and desire, it gained the capacity to play out the media swaps between the textual, visual, theatrical, and sculptural modes. For all their intricate and unexpected temporal and spatial enactments, the intermedia figures materialize and perform the double meaning of excess as offered by *OED*: in terms of a noun of action signifying "overstepping of the limits of moderation" and "an instance of departure *from* custom" while also containing (bound to its etymological roots of the Latin verb *excedere*) the "action of going *out* or *forth*" (*OED*, s.v. "excess"; "exceed"). Departing from a stable medium singularity to move *forward*—out to another media modalities—such is the dynamic of forms driven by the affective compounds.

Hence it does not seem off the mark to venture that due to the tendency of affects toward accumulation, combining, and intertwining, notwithstanding the affects that can appear contradictory to each other, artistic media have a capacity to exceed their material, generic, and semantic boundaries. In other words, the affective interaction and, in fact, hybridity, grounded in both their formal and relational qualities, generates a media excess through which individual discursive and nondiscursive forms transform their aesthetic ontologies. Such a media excess—the "intermedia surplus" as it were—is to be found during the moments *when* and at the sites *where* a text ceases to be a mere discursive structure, an image acquires other than purely visible qualities, and a sound overcomes its uniquely aural condition, thus amplifying the hybrid movement of forms which simply do not care about their aesthetic purity. And this is also why I propose that inasmuch as the performative force of affects needs to be thought relationally, the aesthetic forms and cultural objects should be considered intermedially, not so much as a transfer from one firmly established media carrier to another but as a movement between manifold media modalities and their mutual transformation.

Such a plea for thinking the media configurations in relation to the tendency of affects to accumulate within the work of aesthetic forms echoes the recent calls for a fundamental *hybridity* of media in general. For what Vinzenz Hediger and Miriam De Rosa notice about an essential impurity of cinema which, from its very beginning, has always already been a "medium in permanent transformation" (2016: 11) holds true for literary forms as well. In his compelling take on the post-media field of the "hybrid moving images," Jihoon Kim elaborates the notion of intermediality not only as "a type of configuration based on the mixture of the components from more than two media and thus on their co-presence and interrelation" but also as a useful concept attuned to "the interactions between different art forms or disciplines," including "dialogue, cohabitation, exchange, transformation, collision, appropriation, and repurposing" (2016: 35–6). To examine the affective interactions and operations across precisely thus construed intermedia relations is the task of any future research that will take seriously the link between the formal work of affects and the affective work of forms.

However, to follow this intermedia dynamic one should not linger uniquely with the appeal of the contemporary digital culture underlaid by the so-called post-media condition—an era in which any notion of medium specificity dissolves in favor of the new media hybridity. Rather, one should also turn to the "ur-concept" of the intermedia thinking, the Bakhtinian *intertextuality*: a productive clash between and a constant mutually transforming dialogue of disparate cultural texts understood as "living utterances" that "cannot fail to brush up against thousands of living dialogic threads, woven by socio-cultural consciousness and around the given object of an utterance" (Bakhtin 1981: 276). Such a multitude, co-presence, and overlapping of mutually clashing voices comes out as a defining feature of the affectively driven generative deformations that this book tried to investigate under the name of disformations.[1] If we want to do justice to the aesthetic force that has a capacity to rewrite form to a new formation through deformation, it seems useful to change vocabulary and to talk about performative mechanisms instead of ways of representation, to focus more on affective operations triggered by forms and less on emotional effects done to the affected subject, and to scrutinize various intermedia figures in their transhistorical movement rather than the allegedly autonomous works of arts.

So really, one might wonder in the end, what happens when forms fall apart? The harmony is gone, a wrong tone takes over, and what we thought we knew begins to move adrift. This is a moment when forms and affects force us to think—disturbingly.

NOTES

Introduction

1 "Truly, one of the enigmas of art, and evidence of the force of its logicality, is that all radical consistency, even that called absurd, culminates in similitude to meaning" (Adorno 2002: 154).

2 All translations from the French, unless otherwise noted, are mine.

3 Thom implicitly builds upon his previous distinction between the "static" and "metabolic" forms as elaborated in his *Structural Stability and Morphogenesis* (1972): "If a static form undergoes an interaction with an external system, the form remains, to begin with, isomorph to itself by virtue of its structural stability," whereas the metabolic form "can have a very complicated topology and is generally fluctuating and very sensitive to perturbations" (2018: 101–2).

4 The 1989 translation by Charles Beecher Hogan and George Kubler (whose third edition is used here) which renders the French word *la courbe* as a semantically flatter "graph" is modified. What remains a highly problematic translational (mis)step is the very title of the book whose English version adds the extra words "in art."

5 I am referring especially to Goethe's *Italian Journey* from 1786–88 (1816–1817/1994) and *The Metamorphosis of Plants* (1790/2009).

6 Bataille was certainly not the first to have considered the notion of the "formless" in relation to the aesthetic forms. Leaving aside the presocratic notion of *apeiron*, referred to as a formless and undifferentiated primordial substance, the major precedent here is Kant with his concept of the sublime (*Erhabene*) that stands for the most radical contrast to the classical idea of beauty. In his *Critique of the Power of Judgement* (1790), the sublime that appears "in its form to be contrapurposive for our power of judgment, unsuitable for our faculty of presentation, and as it were doing violence to our imagination" (2000: 129), is regularly associated with the qualities of being *formlos*. "Only the sublime in nature [. . .] can be considered as entirely formless or shapeless [*formlos oder ungestalt*], but nevertheless as the object of a pure satisfaction, and can demonstrate subjective purposiveness in the given representation" (2000: 160). For a detailed assessment of the notion of the sublime, see Doran 2015. Although not as its main subject, some highly insightful observations on *apeiron* can be found in Harman (2005).

7 My thanks go to Eugenie Brinkema for suggesting this term.

8 A useful overview of affect theory and its various strands is provided in the introduction to Gregg and Seigworth (2010). For an updated

assessment and novel typology of the turn to affect, based no more on the psychological versus philosophical-aesthetic distinction but rather on the different positions and phases in the process of "affective triggering," see van Alphen and Jirsa (2019: 1–14).

9 Importantly, Massumi defines affect in opposition to emotion which stands for "the subjective content, the socio-linguistic fixing of the quality of an experience," and hence for "intensity owned and recognized" (2002: 28).

10 Such a fallacy, Harman asserts, consists in "holding that relations are always liberating and nonrelational realities always reactionary" (2012: 192).

11 In his elaboration of the relational approach, Slaby proposes a key concept of the "affective arrangement" that "comprises an array of persons, things, spaces, discourses, behaviors, expressions or other materials that coalesce into a coordinated formation of mutual *affecting and being-affected*" (Slaby 2019b: 109).

12 I will come later, in Chapter 2 and the final coda, to the interrelated terms of media hybridity and intermediality, as recently developed by Jihoon Kim (2016).

13 The term of the figure has an influential afterlife as put in use and strikingly capitalized by Deleuze in his work on Francis Bacon. Here, the "Figural" is at once derived from Lyotard—in that it is opposed to the "Figurative," an umbrella term including the traditional representation, illustration, and narration—but also inspired by the paintings of Paul Cézanne where the Figural is inseparable from the materialized colors, rhythms, and the work of *sensation*: "the master of deformations, the agent of bodily deformations" (2005: 26). As a result, the "Figure" stands for "the sensible form related to a sensation; it acts immediately upon the nervous system, which is of the flesh" (2005: 25). Despite the influence that Deleuze's appropriation of the term gained in the recent scholarship, the word "figure" will henceforth be used to refer to the sense that Lyotard gives it, that is without any reference to those bodily sensations and with the emphasis on its intermedia oscillation.

Chapter 1

1 Among the important exceptions are Schmitt 2012: 10–11; and Bluhm and Clendenin 2009: 93–6. For an excellent account of the popular, medical, and bioethical debates following the transplant, see Pearl (2017: 88–122).

2 From Abel Gance's antiwar film *J'accuse* (1919) with direct sequences of *gueules cassées*, through Georges Franju's cult horror movie *Eyes Without a Face* (*Les yeux sans visage*, 1960) displaying in an exceptionally gory manner the surgical facial removal along with the bloody faceless flesh

beneath, to the Japanese horror movies such as *Ringu* (Hideo Nakata, 1998) and *Ju On: The Grudge* (dir. Takashi Shimizu, 2002) wherein trauma or curse blurs faces in photos, to the science fiction film *Under the Skin* (dir. Jonathan Glazer, 2013) at the end of which the otherworldly female protagonist extricates her body and face from the skin—the cinematic fascination with the face as a distorted, removable, and destructible object seems omnipresent. In the context of the visual representation of *gueules cassées*, among much discussed works are those by Otto Dix, especially his highly grotesque painting *Die Skatspieler* (The Skat Players, 1920), as well as drawings by Max Beckmann and George Grosz that depict not only the facially mutilated veterans but also their difficult coming to terms with the postwar society. An illuminating account of the facially injured soldiers' visual representation in interwar arts is provided by Gehrhardt (2015: 216–36). In the context of literary expressionism, the mesmerizing images of the disfigured face appear especially in Gottfried Benn's poems "Little Aster" and "Fine Youth" from his 1912 *Morgue* collection (1972), in Georg Trakl's presumably last poem "Grodek" from 1914 (2017), and in John Dos Passos' 1921 novel *Three Soldiers* (1932).

3   A similar point that subject's corporeality "is no longer able to secure the boundary between self and environment," is made by Andreas Huyssen (2015: 43). In contrast, Dana Amir's psychoanalytical account posits that the image of the faceless head provides a metaphor for language striving to reach the "insufferable interior" (2014: 21).

4   My use of the distinction draws on the work of Didi-Huberman. Whereas the *visible* stands for what manifests itself while being tangible, material, and related to its representation as a product of an event, the *visual* embraces symptomatic events reaching the visible indexically, including their transfiguration (2005: 11–31). The analogical distinction is then elaborated in his contrasting terms of the "figured figures" (*figures figurées*) and "figuring figures" (*figures figurantes*). While the former denotes the "figure fixed as representational object," the latter signifies the process of "what might become visible" (2005: 141).

5   In what is thus far the most comprehensive analytical study of the novel and its diverse adaptations, Jerrold E. Hogle observes that Leroux "emphatically continues the Gothic tradition both by employing quasi-antiquated settings and ghostlike figures to abject middle-class anxieties and by extending the foundations of both the Gothic and opera in its simulation of the already counterfeit" (2002: 107).

6   "[I]t disavows it by combining into one two quite different elements that undermine the established bourgeois order, aristocratic decadence and the coming proletarian subversion" (Žižek 1991: 62).

7   For a detailed reading of Leroux's novel through Kristevian concept of "abject," see Hogle (2002: 51–4).

8   "Oh! oui, *vivrais-je cent ans*, j'entendrais toujours la clameur surhumaine qu'il poussa, le cri de sa douleur et de sa rage infernales, pendant que la

chose apparaissait à mes yeux immenses d'horreur, comme ma *bouche*
qui ne se refermait pas et qui cependant *ne criait plus*" (Leroux 2008: 132;
emphasis added).

9 A similar point is made by van Alphen (1993: 105–13) who, in his
   affective reading of Bacon's work, analyzes the portraits of the Pope
   Innocent X against the background of the "conflict between narrativity
   and non-narrativity that situates death in the living body, rather than as a
   final event after life" (1993: 97).

10 The "intentional affect" falls under Brinkema's elaborated critique of what
   she phrases as the "new intentional fallacy," that is, a phenomenologically
   driven assertion "that each instance of cinematic affect is of or related to
   a spectator, that affect by definition represents or gives over something as
   some thing to an other." Against such a fallacy, she poses a notion of affect
   that "is non-intentional, indifferent, and resists the given-over attributes of
   a teleological spectatorship with acquirable gains" (2014: 33).

11 For a brilliant assessment of this analogy, based on the structure of shell
   shock, see Zusi 2012. A more general introduction to Weiner's early prose
   is provided by Thomas (1995: 105–15).

12 For all this acknowledgment and the current increase of Weiner
   scholarship in Czech, German, and English, most of his short stories and
   novels, however, have yet to be translated into English (with the recent
   exception of *The Game for Real*, 2015). All quotes from Weiner's text are
   my translations from the Czech.

13 Along with Freud's and Weiner's text, the history of the face crossed
   another important threshold in 1919, when Rudolf Kassner published
   his book *Zahl und Gesicht* (Number and Face), wherein he develops his
   concept of a dynamic physiognomics, countering the traditional principle
   of identity coming between the external (body) and the internal (soul).
   For an insightful account of Kassner's work, see Gray (2004: 167–202).

14 The thorough analytical and contextual studies of both Bataille's entry
   on the formless and the revue *Documents* (1929–1930) are provided by
   Hollier (1991; 1992), Didi-Huberman (1995), and Crowley and Hegarty,
   eds. (2005).

15 As precisely argued by Douglas Smith, the notion of the formless
   offers "a useful instrument for the analysis of art located at the edges of
   recognizable form, where the figurative remains stubbornly visible in its
   disfigurement" (2005: 228).

16 Deleuze and Guattari use both terms when referring to the politics of
   the face as a "strong organization" constituted by "the faciality traits":
   "Dismantling the face is the same as breaking through the wall of signifier
   and getting out of the black hole of subjectivity" (2004: 128, 208).

17 As documented by the letters he sent to his parents from the battlefront
   in Serbia in January 1915, Weiner suffered a nervous breakdown and was
   subsequently demobilized. For more details, see Widera (2001: 47).

Notes 123

18 In recent years, a growing scholarly interest in the phenomenon of
gueules cassées has included disciplines such as cultural history, sociology,
psychology, visual and disability studies, owing much to the pioneering
work of Sophie Delaporte (1996). For a thorough cultural study of *gueules
cassées* as the "powerful walking reminders of the war" (21) throughout
Germany, France, and Great Britain from the point of view of both the
wounded and the onlooker, see Gehrhardt 2015. The images of the facial
disfigurements are further explored as "a symbol and consequence of
industrialized war" (17) from the interdisciplinary point of view by
Biernoff (2017).

19 For a close examination of Rémi's pacifist memoirs, see Gerhardt (2015:
52–62).

20 A similar point is made by Gehrhardt: "The onlooker, whether the
disfigured man—who struggles to reconcile the image reflected in the
mirror with his face as he has always known it—or an external 'other,'
experiences conflicting impulses towards identification, on the one hand,
and distance, on the other" (2015: 25).

Chapter 2

1 See, for instance, the early poem "Temno-sinie oboi . . . " (Dark-blue
wallpaper . . .) from his 1918 collection *Two Paths*, or his novels *King,
Queen, Knave* (1928) and *The Gift* (1938).

2 For a more detailed account of the wallpaper occurrences in Nabokov's
work, see Morris 2011: 285–300.

3 My point here is not to unfairly criticize the certainly meritorious, albeit
at places, incomplete 1973 English translation of the groundbreaking
Vocabulaire de la psychanalyse by Laplanche and Pontalis (1967) but I
see no good reason for converting a clear definition of the phantasm
as "[s]cénario imaginaire où le sujet est présent [. . .]" (2007: 152) into
an overtly interpretative "[i]maginary scene in which the subject is
protagonist [. . .]" (1988: 314). Therefore, I bring the translation back to
its original sense of the "scenario" containing the meanings of a script, a
screenplay, and an outline of a play.

4 The conspicuous analogy between the "evil designer" and the narrator
was noted by many Nabokov scholars. Pushing this observation further,
however, Adam Weinar points out that the very metatextual "alas"
inside the parentheses reveals the narrator's (or rather implied author's)
resentment at the possibility that he would be identified with the "dreadful
inventor" (1998: 191–2).

5 A proper description of the rococo style and its contemporary revival
would take us well beyond the limits of this chapter, so let me just refer
to the few groundbreaking works to which my approach owes much.

For the origins and development of the rococo style, see Bailey 2014: 8–22); and Berchtold, Démoris, and Martin, eds. (2012); for rococo as a fundamentally intermedial and transhistorical aesthetic style, see Sypher (1960); Weisgerber (1991); Ireland (2006); and Coffin (2008).

6 An important precedent to the playful rococo style that remains surprisingly overlooked by art-historian scholarship is the ornamental *Kwab* style that flourished during the seventeenth century mainly in the northern Netherlands and whose importance was recently charted by the eponymous exhibition at Rijksmuseum in Amsterdam. Blending grotesque forms into each other and morphing the seashells, monsters, and human bodies into the liquid amorphous formations that wave over various objects of decorative arts, *Kwab* substantially pre-echoes the subversive *rocaille* qualities. For a useful introduction to the *Kwab* style, see Baarssen (2018).

7 Harries draws here on the leading rococo scholar Hermann Bauer's book *Rocaille: Zur Herkunft und zum Wesen eines Ornament-Motivs* (Rocaille: Toward the Origin and Character of Some Ornamental Motifs, 1962) and points out that Bauer "ties the origin of rocaille to the development of French grotesque ornament, a characteristic of which is the joining of two different spatial logics, one ornamental, the other pictorial. The grotesque depends on that oscillation between picture and ornament" (1983: 22).

8 For this overtly Kantian reiteration, see, for instance, the entry "Orner/ Ornement/Ornemental" in the renowned and many times reedited *Vocabulaire d'esthétique* by Étienne Souriau: "To ornament (orner) means to add external components to something for the purpose of embellishing its appearance. An ornament is thus an additional element. The two features that define the ornament are the following: (1) its purpose that consists in enhancing the already finished work, and (2) its non-functional character within the very structure of the work" (2004: 1100).

9 For the analysis of Meissonnier's engravings I am relying on the 1969 reprint of *Livre d'ornemens*, edited and introduced by Dorothea Nyberg. For a useful account of his engravings, see Ankersmit (2005: 289–99).

10 Although the subversive rococo curves counter the Kantian view in many respects, it is fair to note that it was precisely Kant who laid ground for this nonrepresentational view of ornament when claiming that "designs *à la grecque*, foliage for borders or on wallpaper, etc., signify nothing by themselves: they do not represent anything, no object under a determinate concept, and are free beauties" (2000: 114).

11 See, for example, Ireland (2006: 98), and Pomerantz (2009: 16–24). In this respect, Menninghaus argues that Kantian foliage on wallpaper "should be seen more as a parergonal ornamentation of rooms rather than as an absolute decorative pattern" (229n63).

12 For the relationship between the visual structure of ornament and the ornamental rhythm of hallucinatory states during schizophrenia, see Navratil (1978: 29–31).

13 For an overview of this canonical scholarly pattern I cannot but refer to the carefully annotated bibliography provided by Catherine Golden (2004). A highly useful comment on the feminist but also racial, ethnic, postcolonial, and sexual interpretations of Gilman's short story can be found in Allen (2009: 19–25). Another frequent tendency is to read the diegetic wallpaper as a screen for all kinds of projections and visions, be they political and social (Doran 2013: 73–9), or hysterical (Jacobus 2014). For a brilliant biographical reading of the story, see Horowitz (2010: 173–210).

14 I am referring primarily to this passage: "Does not the paradox of repetition lie in the fact that one can speak of repetition only by virtue of the change or difference that it introduces into the mind which contemplates it? By virtue of a difference that the mind *draws from* repetition?" (Deleuze 2004: 90).

15 I am using the term "hybrid moving images" in line with Kim who explains them as a conceptual field containing "an array of impure image forms characterized by the interrelation of the material, technical, and aesthetic components" of mutually influencing audiovisual media (2016: 3, 35).

16 Since the English translation "the *all-over* fold" (Deleuze 2006: 141) cannot obviously retain the original bilingual dynamic, I am quoting from the French. For an insightful elaboration of the Deleuzian fold, see Bal (2003) who follows the intermedia and no less transhistorical "language of the baroque fold" that dissolves the boundary between the body and drapery by its endless frilling from Bernini's *The Ecstasy of St. Theresa* (1652) to the biomorphic sculptures by Louise Bourgeois from the late 1960s.

Chapter 3

1 Two years later, Žižek specifies that the "properly aesthetic attitude of a radical ecologist is not that of admiring or longing for a pristine nature of virgin forests and clear sky, but rather that of accepting waste as such, of discovering the aesthetic potential of waste, of decay, of the inertia of rotten material which serves no purpose" (2010: 35).

2 I am alluding especially to the pioneering work of Jane Bennett (2010) whose take on diverse events, including the "experience of litter," considered as "encounters between ontologically diverse actants, some human, some not, though all thoroughly material" (2010: xiv) is particularly useful for thinking the mediality of the garbage.

3 See especially Petit (1991: 62–74); Platten (1999: 113–129); and Maclean (2003).

4 As he explains in his "intellectual autobiography" *The Wind Spirit* (*Le Vent Paraclet*, 1977), see Tournier (1988: 250).

5 For a more detailed account of this critique, see Petit (1991: 47–49); and Bevan (1986: 7–9).

6 The passage in question goes as follows: "*I suffer from constipation* but I should be cured if I could have the face of a heterosexual to cover with my dung each morning. To shit on a heterosexual. But perhaps even that is doing him too much honor? Isn't my shit pure gold compared to his baseness?" (Tournier 1998: 103).

7 For a comprehensive overview of the scholarship on waste and garbage within the humanities, see Foote and Mazzolini (2012: 8–13); Lindner and Meissner (2016: 4–12). From the perspective of media archaeology and theory the theme has been rather neglected; among the recent exceptions are Gabrys (2013); Lewe, Othold, and Oxen, eds. (2016), and Rabaté (2018).

8 Despite various attempts to distinguish waste from garbage and trash, the distinction remains blurred. As Greg Kennedy notes, "[w]hereas waste results from a relative, subjective devaluation, technological objectification, that is unconditional, absolute devaluation, engenders trash." Unlike the waste, he further argues, the trash and garbage belong to the "objects presupposed as essentially disposable" (2012: 10, 23).

9 Among the most insightful instances of this approach are Gee (2009); Morrison (2015); and Dini (2016).

10 See especially Viney (2014: 151–164) and Dini (143–179). Given the thematic and narrative dominance of the garbage in Tournier's novel, it is surprising that *Gemini* is usually only briefly referred to by scholars drawing on the waste studies. See, for instance, Harpet (1998: 481–482, 485), Dini (13–14, 101), and Moser (2002: 94–95).

11 Although slightly different in the object of its study, this approach is close to Jean-Michel Rabaté's recent take on rust. In his dominantly materialist reading of the generative corrosions produced by the rust, he shows how this byproduct is "not a burden or a blemish but a mode of expression combining ethics and aesthetics" (2018: 21).

12 Describing the sexual focus of his book, Tournier aptly noted: "A hundred years ago it was a bold stroke to call homosexuality by its name in a novel. The bold stroke in Gemini was to call heterosexuality by its name" (1988: 219).

13 To somewhat moderate this enthusiastic view, it is worth mentioning the Brazilian anti-anthropocentric short film *Isle of Flowers* (dir. Jorge Furtado, 1989). In a highly sarcastic manner, a different definition of the garbage, based on not only a completely one-sided relationship of humans to their environment but also a peculiar capacity of the privileged society

to *trash* the rest of the population is provided by the voice-off narrator who states: "Garbage is everything that human beings produce as a result of the combined efforts of the highly developed telencephalon and the opposable thumb and which, in a judgment of one human being, is not fit to be made into sauce."

14 For a further theoretical elaboration of this approach, see Shanks, Platt, and Rathje (2004).

15 It is worth noting that Tournier's description of this place close to Miramas corresponds to the well-known locality Entressen dans la Crau which stands for the largest garbage dump in Europe since its foundation in 1912 (cf. de Silguy 2009: 139).

16 For an excellent theoretical elaboration of this notion in terms of a conceptual interface that interconnects and operates between two objects, see Dubois (1999: 11–24). The theoretical, cultural, and historical implications of Auerbach's *figura* are comprehensively described by Porter (2017).

17 The translation of this fragment comes from Gille (2007: 39).

18 For a fundamental influence of the modern French thought (especially Lévi-Strauss' anthropology) on Tournier's oeuvre, see, for instance, Worton (1992: 111) and Bracker (2001: 75).

19 As much as Ann Carter's translation is precise, an important aspect goes missing here. While the French original is rather implicit about the "infinite repetitions" of the copies, it is explicit about the objects' "infinite power": "Non sans mětre exalté avant leur inhumation devant *la puissance infinie* de ces objets produits en masse – et donc copies de copies de copies de copies de copies de copies, etc" (2011: 103; emphasis added).

20 In his argument, Deleuze draws primarily on Klossowski's 1958 article and his conference paper (1967).

21 A similar point is made by Susan Petit who observes that Alexandre "attacks Platonism" in favor of a more materialist Aristotelianism (1991: 69–70).

22 This should not imply, however, that OOO would overlook processes of mediation. In his recent book, Harman clearly argues quite the opposite: "Against the assumptions of common sense, objects cannot make *direct* contact with each other, but require a third term or mediator for such contact to occur." (Harman 2018: 12). For a more sustained discussion of the nonrelational conception of the reality of objects and the Heideggerian-inspired term of the radical "withdrawal," see especially Harman (2005 and 2011).

Chapter 4

1 To make her case, Weiss is building upon Max Imdahl's notion of the nonmimetic "dissimilar portrait" (1988) coined in relation to Giacometti's drawings.

2   The translation of this fragment is by Peter Zusi whose essay on Weiner is
    discussed later.
3   See especially Widera (2001: 73), and Málek (2008: 83).
4   A detailed biographical reading of both paintings is provided in Collins
    (2001: 160–214). An overview of the influential philosophical accounts
    of the diptych of empty chairs by Jaspers, Heidegger, Bataille, and
    Merleau-Ponty is to be found in Nichols (ed. 2017). For the genesis of and
    correspondence describing the diptych I rely on Pickvance (1984: 235,
    263).
5   I borrow and slightly modify the phrase "metonymic self-portrait" from
    Craig Owens who, with reference to Meyer Schapiro, describes van Gogh's
    painting *A Pair of Shoes* (1886) as "a (displaced or metonymic) self-
    portrait" (1992: 94).
6   As was the case in Chapter 2, the translation here is modified and instead
    of the phrase "memory traces" (1988: 482) I put here—in line with, for
    instance, Rabaté (2014: 140)—the more accurate term of the "mnesic
    traces" (*traces mnésiques*) (Laplanche and Pontalis 2009: 121).
7   For an insightful account on the role of chairs in Schiele's work, especially
    on the poster where "two opened books join the scream of the chairs
    that demand to be used. Their cry is so powerful that enough presence
    is conferred upon the chairs to use themselves," see Escalera (2011: 161).
    For a thorough reading of Salcedo's Istanbul installation, see Bal (2010:
    218–240) and Lauzon (2017: 106–122).
8   I borrow the phrase "chair anatomy" (*une anatomie de la chaise*) from
    Conte who points out that "with its back(rest), arm(rests), legs, and feet,
    the chair reveals its anthropomorphic character" (2013: 126).
9   "The whole of Literature can declare *Larvatus prodeo*, As I walk forward, I
    point out my mask." (Barthes 1970: 40). It remains to add, however, that in
    art and literature, no true face is hiding beneath the mask, but just another
    mask. And what is more, the gesture of pointing out the mask can very
    well be part of the whole aesthetic "masquerade."
10 For some reason, the English translation completely omits this highly
    important stage direction.
11 For an insightful account of the aesthetically generative "nothing" and the
    ways it shapes the forms of literary narrative, see Vicks (2015).
12 Analyzing the language of the play, Elizabeth Klaver notices an important
    analogy between the absence of the guests and the absence of language
    itself (1989: 523–524). However, while she claims that the "language
    tries to cover its own absence by filling up the void, yet the void tends to
    empty the language by producing holes in the discourse" (1989: 525), my
    argument is that rather than an ontological void, the language of the play
    takes up the formal work of the empty chairs that generate the presence of
    the absence.

13 A contextual and, indeed, fruitful occurrence cannot go unmentioned here. Some dozen meters from and a few steps below Bigelmayr's sculpture is situated a meeting point of IKKM (Internationales Kolleg für Kulturtechnikforschung und Medienphilosophie) that can be rightly called the heart of (not only) German *Medienwissenschaft*. Between April 2008 and March 2020, IKKM in Weimar hosted outstanding scholars from all over the world who developed here in joint discussion and coordinated work new connections between cultural techniques and media philosophy.

Coda

1 In a recent superb reflection on Bakhtin's conceptual toolbox, especially his terms of double-voicedness and polyphonicity that he elaborated in his readings of the novels by Fyodor Dostoyevsky, Rey Chow argues for a generative clash that is fully in line with the present reading of the affective operations: "Insofar as the doubled-voiced or polyphonic utterance is, rather than a space of unison and harmony, an echo chamber, an opening for a strife for dominance, the voice (as enunciation) in Bakhtin's reading is partial, interferential, an internally split" (2019: 124).

BIBLIOGRAPHY

Adorno, Theodor W. *Aesthetic Theory*, edited by Gretel Adorno and Rolf Tiedemann; translated by Robert Hullot-Kentor. London and New York: Continuum, 2002.

Allen, Judith A. *The Feminism of Charlotte Perkins Gilman: Sexualities, Histories, Progressivism*. Chicago: University of Chicago Press, 2009.

Alphen, Ernst van. *Francis Bacon and the Loss of Self*. Cambridge, MA: Harvard University Press, 1993.

Alphen, Ernst van. *Art in Mind: How Contemporary Images Shape Thought*. Chicago: University of Chicago Press, 2005.

Alphen, Ernst van. "Affective Operations of Art and Literature." *RES: Anthropology and Aesthetics*, no. 53/54 (2008): 21–30.

Alphen, Ernst van. "Reading for Affect: Francis Bacon and the Work of Sensation." In *How to Do Things with Affects: Affective Triggers in Aesthetic Forms and Cultural Practices*, edited by Ernst van Alphen and Tomáš Jirsa, 163–76. Leiden: Brill, 2019.

Alphen, Ernst van, and Tomáš Jirsa, eds. "Introduction: Mapping Affective Operations." In *How to Do Things with Affects: Affective Triggers in Aesthetic Forms and Cultural Practices*, 1–14. Leiden: Brill, 2019.

Amir, Dana. *Cleft Tongue: The Language of Psychic Structures*, translated by Mirjam Hadar. London: Karnac Books, 2014.

Ankersmit, Frank. "Rococo as the Dissipation of Boredom." In *Compelling Visuality: The Work of Art in and out of History*, edited by Claire Farrago and Robert Zwijneberg, 132–55. Minneapolis: University of Minnesota Press, 2003.

Ankersmit, Frank. *Sublime Historical Experience*. Stanford, CA: Stanford University Press, 2005.

Aristotle. *Physics*, translated by Robin Waterfield. New York: Oxford University Press, 1996

Atmani, Isabelle. "Une clinique de l'informe: De la défiguration à la monstruosité." *Recherche en Psychanalyse* 1, no. 3 (2005): 75–84.

Auerbach, Erich. "Figura." In *Scenes from the Drama of European Literature: Six Essays*, edited by Wlad Godzich and Jochen Schulte-Sasse; translated by Ralph Manheim, 11–76. Minneapolis: University of Minnesota Press, 1984 [1938].

Aumont, Jacques. *À quoi pensent les films*. Paris: Séguier, 1996.

Baarssen, Reinier. *Kwab: Ornament as Art in the Age of Rembrandt*. Amsterdam: Rijskmuseum, 2018.

Bailey, Gauvin Alexander. *The Spiritual Rococo: Decor and Divinity from the Salons of Paris to the Missions of Patagonia*. Burlington: Ashgate, 2014.

Bakhtin, Mikhail M. *Dialogic Imagination: Four Essays*, edited by Michael Holquist; translated by Caryl Emerson. Austin: University of Texas Press, 1981.

Bal, Mieke. *Travelling Concepts in the Humanities: A Rough Guide*. Toronto: University of Toronto Press, 2002.

Bal, Mieke. "Ecstatic Aesthetics: Metaphoring Bernini," In *Compelling Visuality: The Work of Art in and Out of History*, edited by Claire Farrago and Robert Zwijneberg, 1–30. Minneapolis: University of Minnesota Press, 2003.

Bal, Mieke. *Of What One Cannot Speak: Doris Salcedo's Political Art*. Chicago: University of Chicago Press, 2010.

Barthes, Roland. *Writing Degree Zero*, translated by Annette Lavers and Colin Smith. Boston: Beacon Press, 1970 [1953].

Barthes, Roland. *A Lover's Discourse: Fragments*, translated by Richard Howard. London: Vintage, 2002 [1977].

Bataille, Georges. *Visions of Excess: Selected Writings 1927–1939*, edited and translated by Allan Stoekl. Minneapolis: University of Minnesota Press, 1985.

Bataille, Georges. *The Accursed Share: An Essay on General Economy. Vol. 1: Consumption*, translated by Robert Hurley. New York: Zone Books, 1988 [1949].

Bauer, Hermann. *Rocaille. Zur Herkunft und zum Wesen eines Ornament-Motivs*, Berlin: Walter de Gruyter, 1962.

Belting, Hans. *Art History after Modernism*, translated by Caroline Saltzwedel, Mitch Cohen, and Kenneth Nortcott. Chicago: The University of Chicago Press, 2003 [1995].

Belting, Hans. *An Anthropology of Images: Picture, Medium, Body*, translated by Thomas Dunlap. Princeton: Princeton University Press, 2011 [2001].

Belting, Hans. *Face and Mask: A Double History*, translated by Thomas S. Hansen and Abby J. Hansen. Princeton: Princeton University Press, 2017 [2013].

Benn, Gottfried. *The Unreconstructed Expressionist*, edited and translated by James M. Ritchie. London: Oswald Wolff, 1972.

Bennett, Jane. *Vibrant Matter: A Political Ecology of Things*. Durham: Duke University Press, 2010.

Bennett, Jill. *Empathic Vision. Affect, Trauma, and Contemporary Art*. Stanford: Stanford University Press, 2005.

Berchtold, Jacques, René Démoris, and Christophe Martin, eds. *Violences du rococo*. Pessac: Presses Universitaires de Bordeaux, 2012.

Bergman, Ingmar. *Three Films: Through a Glass Darkly, Winter Light, The Silence*, translated by Paul Britten. New York: Grove Press, 1970.

Bergson, Henri. *Matter and Memory*, translated by N. M. Paul and W. S. Palmer, New York: Zone Books, 1991 [1896].

Bergson, Henri. *Creative Evolution*, translated by Arthur Mitchell. New York: Dover, 1998 [1907].

Bevan, David. *Michel Tournier*. Amsterdam: Rodopi, 1986.

Biernoff, Suzannah. *Portraits of Violence: War and the Aesthetics of Disfigurement*. Ann Arbor: University of Michigan Press, 2017.

Bluhm, Carla, and Nathan Clendenin. *Someone Else's Face in the Mirror: Identity and the New Science of Face Transplants*. Westport: Praeger, 2009.

Bois, Yve-Alain, and Rosalind E. Krauss. *Formless: A User's Guide*. New York: Zone Books, 1997.

Bois, Yve-Alain, Denis Hollier, Rosalind Krauss, and Hubert Damisch. "A Conversation with Hubert Damisch," *October* 85 (Summer 1998): 3–17.

Boyd, Brian. *Vladimir Nabokov: The American Years*. Princeton: Princeton University Press, 1991.

Bracker, Nicole. "Michel Tournier and the Garbage Heap: Economy in Limbo," *Parallax* 7, no. 2 (2001): 66–80.

Braidotti, Rosi. *The Posthuman*. Cambridge: Polity Press, 2013.

Brinkema, Eugenie. *The Forms of the Affects*. Durham and London: Duke University Press, 2014.

Casetti, Francesco. *The Lumière Galaxy: Seven Key Words for the Cinema to Come*. New York: Columbia University Press, 2015.

Chow, Rey. "Listening after Acousmaticity: Notes on a Transdisciplinary Problematic." In *Sound Objects*, edited by James A. Steintrager and Rey Chow, 113–29. Durham and London: Duke University Press, 2019.

Císař, Karel, ed. *Jan Šerých se narodil 24. 6. 2083 minus jedna; Jan Šerých Was Born on 24. 6. 2083 Minus One*. Prague: Tranzit, 2008.

Císař, Karel. *Věci, o kterých s nikým nemluvím: Současné české umění; 5. Bienále mladého umění Zvon 2005; 6. Bienále mladého umění Zvon 2008*. Prague: tranzit.cz, 2010.

Coffin, Sarah. *Rococo: The Continuing Curve, 1730–2008*. New York: Cooper Hewitt, 2008.

Cojean, Annick. "La femme aux deux visages." *Le Monde*, July 6, 2007. Available online: https://www.lemonde.fr/societe/article/2007/07/06/la-pr emiere-greffee-du-visage-raconte-sa-nouvelle-vie_932443_3224.html (Accessed on: March 21, 2019).

Collins, Bradley I. *Van Gogh and Gauguin: Electric Arguments and Utopian Dreams*. Boulder: Westview Press, 2001.

Conte, Pietro, ed. "Prenez une chaise, monsieur Kantor! Théorie et histoire d'un 'monument impossible.'" In *Une absence présente. Figures de l'image mémorielle*, 121–35. Paris: Mimesis France, 2013.

Crowley, Patrick, and Paul Hegarty, eds. *Formless: Ways In and Out of Form*. Bern: Peter Lang, 2005.

Delaporte, Sophie. *Gueules cassées de la grande guerre*. Paris: Agnès Viedot Éditions, 2004.

Deleuze, Gilles. "Spinoza and the Three 'Ethics,'" translated by Daniel W. Smith and Michael A. Greco. In *Essays Critical and Clinical*, 138–51. Minneapolis: University of Minnesota Press, 1997 [1993].

Deleuze, Gilles. *Difference and Repetition*, translated by Paul Patton. New York and London: Continuum, 2004 [1968].

Deleuze, Gilles. *Francis Bacon: The Logic of Sensation*, translated by Daniel W. Smith. London and New York: Continuum, 2005 [1981].

Deleuze, Gilles. *The Fold: Leibniz and the Baroque*, translated by Tom Conley. London and New York: Continuum, 2006 [1988].

Deleuze, Gilles, and Félix Guattari. *A Thousand Plateaus: Capitalism and Schizophrenia*, translated by Brian Massumi. London and New York: Continuum, 2004 [1980].

Derrida, Jacques. *The Truth in Painting*, translated by Geoff Bennington and Ian McLeod. Chicago: University of Chicago Press, 1987 [1978].

Derrida, Jacques. "...That Dangerous Supplement...." In *Of Grammatology*, translated by Gayatri Chakravorty Spivak, 153–78. Baltimore: Johns Hopkins University Press, 2016 [1967].

Didi-Huberman, Georges, ed. "La grammaire, le chahut, le silence: pour une anthropologie du visage." *à visage découvert*, 15–55. Paris: Flammarion, 1992.

Didi-Huberman, Georges. *La Ressemblance informe ou le gai savoir visuel selon Georges Bataille*. Paris: Macula, 1995.

Didi-Huberman, Georges. *Ninfa moderna. Essai sur le drapé tombé*. Paris: Gallimard, 2002.

Didi-Huberman, Georges. *Confronting Images: Questioning the Ends of a Certain History of Art*, translated by John Goodman. Philadelphia: Penn State University Press, 2005 [1990].

Dini, Rachele. *Consumerism, Waste, and Re-Use in Twentieth-Century Fiction: Legacies of the Avant-Garde*. New York: Springer, 2016.

Doran, Robert. *The Theory of the Sublime from Longinus to Kant*. Cambridge: Cambridge University Press, 2015.

Doran, Sabine. *The Culture of Yellow: or The Visual Politics of Late Modernity*. New York: Bloomsbury, 2013.

Dos Passos, John. *Three Soldiers*. New York: The Modern Library, 1932 [1921].

Dubois, Philippe. "La question des Figures à travers les champs du savoir: le savoir de la lexicologie: note sur *Figura* d'Erich Auerbach." In *Figure, figurale*, edited by François Aubral and Dominique Château, 11–24. Paris: L'Harmattan, 1999.

Edeling, Thomas. *L'univers théâtral d'Eugène Ionesco dans l'univers essayiste et politique de François Bondy*. Bern: Peter Lang, 2009.

Engell, Lorenz, and Joseph Vogl. "Vorwort." In *Kursbuch Medienkultur. Die maßgeblichen Theorien von Brecht bis Baudrillard*, edited by Claus Pias et al., 8–11. Stuttgart: DVA, 2002 [1999].

Escalera, Carla Carmona. "*Chairs* as Structures in Egon Schiele's Aesthetics: Egon Schiele's Place in Wittgenstein's Vienna." *Nómadas. Revista Crítica de Ciencias Sociales y Jurídicas* 29, no. 1 (2011): 155–65.

Eyers, Tom. *Speculative Formalism: Literature, Theory, and the Critical Present.*
    Evanston: Northwestern University Press, 2017.
Fédida, Pierre. *Par où commence le corps. Retour sur la régression.* Paris:
    Presses Universitaires de France, 2000.
Fédida, Pierre. "Voir la chair." *Textuel 42: Le Corps de l'informe,* edited by Évelyne
    Grossman, 55–9. Paris: Université de Paris VII—Denis Diderot, 2002.
Focillon, Henri. *La vie des formes.* Paris: Presses Universitaires de France, 1981
    [1934].
Focillon, Henri. *The Life of Forms in Art,* translated by Charles Beecher Hogan
    and George Kubler. New York: Zone Books, 1992 [1934].
Foote, Stephanie, and Elizabeth Mazzolini. *Histories of the Dustheap: Waste,
    Material Cultures, Social Justice.* Cambridge: MIT Press, 2012.
Freud, Sigmund. "The 'Uncanny.'" *The Standard Edition of the Complete
    Psychological Works of Sigmund Freud. Vol. XVII (1917–1919): An Infantile
    Neurosis and Other Works,* edited and translated by James Strachey,
    217–56. London: Hogarth Press, 1955 [1919].
Freud, Sigmund. "Mourning and Melancholia." In *The Standard Edition of
    the Complete Psychological Works of Sigmund Freud, Vol. 14 (1916–1918),*
    edited and translated by James Strachey, 243–58. London: The Hogarth
    Press, 1981 [1917].
Fuller, Matthew. "Pits to Bits: Interview with Graham Harwood," July 2010.
    Available online: http://www.spc.org/fuller/interviews/pits-to-bits-
    interview-with-graham-harwood/.
Gabrys, Jennifer. *Digital Rubbish: A Natural History of Electronics.* Ann Arbor:
    University of Michigan Press, 2013.
Gado, Frank. *The Passion of Ingmar Bergman.* Durham: Duke University Press,
    2007.
Gauguin, Paul. *Avant et après.* Paris: La Table Ronde, 1994 [1903].
Gee, Sophie. *Making Waste: Leftovers and the Eighteenth-Century Imagination.*
    Princeton: Princeton University Press, 2009.
Gehrhardt, Marjorie. *The Men with Broken Faces: Gueules Cassées of the First
    World War.* Bern: Peter Lang, 2015.
Gervais, Bertrand, and Audrey Lemieux, eds. "A la rencontre du lisible et du
    visible." In *Perspectives croisées sur la figure: A la rencontre du lisible et du
    visible,* 1–14. Montreal: Presses de l'Université du Québec, 2012.
Gille, Zsuzsa. *From the Cult of Waste to the Trash Heap of History: The
    Politics of Waste in Socialist and Postsocialist Hungary.* Bloomington and
    Indianapolis: Indiana University Press, 2007.
Gilman, Charlotte Perkins. *The Yellow Wall-Paper, Herland, and Selected
    Writings,* edited by Denise D. Knight. New York: Penguin Books, 2009.
Gilman, Sander L. *Creating Beauty to Cure the Soul: Race and Psychology in the
    Shaping of Aesthetic Surgery.* Durham: Duke University Press, 1998.
Goethe, Johann Wolfgang von. *Italian Journey,* translated by Robert R.
    Heitner. In *Collected Works,* vol. 6, edited by Thomas P. Saine and Jeffrey L.
    Sammons. Princeton, NJ: Princeton University Press, 1994 [1816].

Goethe, Johann Wolfgang von. *The Metamorphosis of Plants*, edited by Gordon L. Miller and translated by Douglas Miller, Cambridge, MA: MIT Press, 2009 [1790].

Golden, Catherine, ed. *Charlotte Perkins Gilman's The Yellow Wall-Paper: A Sourcebook and Critical Edition*. London: Routledge, 2004.

Golden, Catherine, and Joanna S. Zangrando, eds. *The Mixed Legacy of Charlotte Perkins Gilman*. University of Delaware Press, 2000.

Grabar, Oleg. *The Mediation of Ornament*. Washington: Princeton University Press, 1992.

Gray, Richard T. *About Face: German Physiognomic Thought from Lavater to Auschwitz*. Detroit: Wayne State University Press, 2004.

Gregg, Melissa, and Gregory J. Seigworth, eds. "An Inventory of Shimmers." In *The Affect Theory Reader*, 1–26. Durham and London: Duke University Press, 2010.

Gumbrecht, Hans Ulrich. *Atmosphere, Mood, Stimmung: On a Hidden Potential of Literature*, translated by Erik Butler. Stanford: Stanford University Press, 2012 [2011].

Hanich, Julian. "Review of Eugenie Brinkema: *The Forms of the Affects*." *Projections: The Journal for Movies and Mind* 9, no. 1 (2015): 112–17.

Hansen, Mark. "Affect as Medium, or the 'Digital-Facial-Image.'" *Journal of Visual Culture* 2, no. 2 (2003): 205–28.

Harman, Graham. *Guerrilla Metaphysics: Phenomenology and the Carpentry of Things*. Chicago: Open Court, 2005.

Harman, Graham. *Prince of Networks: Bruno Latour and Metaphysics*. Melbourne: re.press, 2009.

Harman, Graham. *The Quadruple Object*. Winchester, England: Zero Books, 2011.

Harman, Graham. "The Well-Wrought Broken Hammer: Object Oriented Literary Criticism." *New Literary History* 43, no. 2 (2012): 183–203.

Harman, Graham. *Object-Oriented Ontology: A New Theory of Everything*. London: Pelican Books, 2018.

Harpet, Cyrille. *Du déchet: Philosophie des immondices, corps, ville industrie*. Paris: L'Harmattan, 1998.

Harries, Karsten. *The Bavarian Rococo Church: Between Faith and Aestheticism*. New Haven: Yale University Press, 1983.

Harries, Karsten. *The Broken Frame: Three Lectures*. Washington: Catholic University of America Press, 1989.

Hediger, Vinzenz, and Miriam De Rosa. "Post-What? Post-When? A Conversation on the 'Posts' of Post-Media and Post-Cinema." *Cinéma&Cie* 16, no. 26/27 (2016): 9–20.

Herzogenrath, Bernd, ed. "Media Matter: An Introduction." In *Media Matter: The Materiality of Media, Matter as Medium*, 1–16. London and New York: Bloomsbury, 2015.

Herzogenrath, Bernd, "Et in Academia Ego: Affect and Academic Writing." In *How to Do Things with Affects: Affective Triggers in Aesthetic Forms and*

Cultural Practices, edited by Ernst van Alphen and Tomáš Jirsa, 216–34. Leiden: Brill, 2019.

Hicks, Dan. "The Material-Cultural Turn: Event and Effect." In *The Oxford Handbook of Material Culture Studies*, edited by Dan Hicks and Mary Beaudry, 25–98. Oxford: Oxford University Press, 2010.

Hochman, Barbara. "The Reading Habit and 'The Yellow Wallpaper.'" *American Literature* 74, no. 1 (2002): 89–110.

Hogle, Jerrold E. *The Undergrounds of the Phantom of the Opera: Sublimation and the Gothic in Leroux's Novel and Its Progeny*. New York: Palgrave, 2002.

Hollier, Denis. "La Valeur d'usage de l'impossible." *Documents* 1, VII–XXXIV. Paris: Jean-Michel Place, 1991.

Hollier, Denis. *Against Architecture: The Writings of Georges Bataille*, translated by Betsy Wing. Cambridge and London: MIT Press, 1992.

Horn, Eva. "Editor's Introduction: 'There are no media.'" *Grey Room* 8, no. 29 (2007): 7–13.

Horowitz, Helen L. *Wild Unrest: Charlotte Perkins Gilman and the Making of The Yellow Wall-Paper*. New York: Oxford University Press, 2010.

Huyssen, Andreas. *Miniature Metropolis: Literature in an Age of Photography and Film*. Cambridge and London: Harvard University Press, 2015.

Imdahl, Max. "Relationen zwischen Porträt und Individuum." In *Individualität. Poetik und Hermeneutik* 13, edited by Manfred Frank and Anselm Haverkamp, 587–98. Munich: Wilhelm Fink, 1988.

Ingold, Tim. *The Perception of the Environment: Essays on Livelihood, Dwelling and Skill*. London: Routledge, 2000.

Ionesco, Eugène. *Four Plays: The Bald Soprano, The Lesson, Jack; or, The Submission, The Chairs*, translated by Donald M. Allen, New York: Grove Press, 1958.

Ionesco, Eugène. *Théâtre Complet*. Paris: Gallimard, 1991.

Ireland, Ken. *Cythera Regained: The Rococo Revival in European Literature and the Arts, 1830–1910*. Madison: Fairleigh Dickinson University Press, 2006.

Iversen, Margaret. *Beyond Pleasure: Freud, Lacan, Barthes*. University Park: Pensylvania State University Press, 2007.

Jacobus, Mary. "An Unnecessary Maze of Sign-Reading." In *Readers and Reading*, edited by Andrew Bennett, 94–111. New York and London: Routledge, 2014.

Jameson, Fredric. *Postmodernism, or, The Cultural Logic of Late Capitalism*. Durham and London: Duke University Press, 1991.

Jirsa, Tomáš. "Lost in Pattern: Rococo Ornament and Its Journey to Contemporary Art through Wallpaper." In *Where Is History Today? New Ways of Representing the Past*, edited by Marcel Arbeit and Ian Christie, 201–19. Olomouc: Palacký University Press, 2015.

Jirsa, Tomáš. "Portrait of Absence: The Aisthetic Mediality of the Empty Chairs." *Zeitschrift für Medien- und Kulturforschung* 7, no. 2 (2016): 13–28.

Jirsa, Tomáš. "Affective Disfigurations: Faceless Encounters between Literary Modernism and the Great War." In *How to Do Things with Affects: Affective Triggers in Aesthetic Forms and Cultural Practices*, edited by Ernst van Alphen and Tomáš Jirsa, 121–42. Leiden: Brill, 2019.

Kafka, Franz. *The Trial*, edited by Ritchie Robertson; translated by Mike Mitchell. Oxford: Oxford University Press, 2009 [1925].

Kant, Immanuel. *Critique of the Power of Judgment*, edited by Paul Guyer; translated by Paul Guyer and Eric Matthews. Cambridge: Cambridge University Press, 2000 [1790].

Kanters, Robert. "Creux et plein d'ordures," *Le Figaro Littéraire*, April 5, 1975: 15–17.

Kennedy, Greg. *An Ontology of Trash: The Disposable and Its Problematic Nature*. Albany: SUNY Press, 2012.

Kim, Jihoon. *Between Film, Video, and the Digital: Hybrid Moving Images in the Post-Media Age*. London and New York: Bloomsbury, 2016.

Kimball, Fiske. *Creation of the Rococo*. Philadelphia: Philadelphia Museum of Art, 1964.

Kittler, Friedrich. *Gramophone, Film, Typewriter*, translated by Geoffrey Winthrop-Young and Michael Wutz. Stanford: Stanford University Press, 1999 [1986].

Klaver, Elizabeth. "The Play of Language in Ionesco's Play of Chairs." *Modern Drama* 32, no. 4 (1989): 521–31.

Klossowski, Pierre. "Nietzsche, le polytheisme et la parodie." *Revue de métaphysique et de morale* 63, no. 2/3 (1958): 325–48.

Klossowski, Pierre. "Oubli et anamnèse dans l'expérience vécue de l'éternel retour du Même." In *Nietzsche: Cahiers de Royaumont Philosophie. No. 6*, 227–35. Paris: Les Éditions de Minuit, 1967.

Kosuth, Joseph. "Art after Philosophy" [1969]. In *Art After Philosophy and After: Collected Writings, 1966–1990*, edited by Gabriele Guercio, 13–32. Cambridge: MIT Press, 1991.

Krämer, Sybille. *Medium, Messenger, Transmission: An Approach to Media Philosophy*, translated by Anthony Enns. Amsterdam: Amsterdam University Press, 2015 [2008].

Lacan, Jacques. "The Dream of Irma's Injection." In *The Seminar of Jacques Lacan, Book II: The Ego in Freud's Theory and in the Technique of Psychoanalysis, 1954–1955*, edited by Jacques-Alain Miller; translated by Sylvana Tomaselli, 146–60. Cambridge: Cambridge University Press, 1988 [1955].

Lacan, Jacques. "The Function and Field of Speech and Language in Psychoanalysis" [1966]. In *Écrits: The First Complete Translation in English*, translated by Bruce Fink, 197–268. New York: Norton, 2006a.

Lacan, Jacques. "The Subversion of the Subject and the Dialectic of Desire in the Freudian Unconscious." In *Écrits: The First Complete Translation in English*, translated by Bruce Fink, 671–702. New York: Norton, 2006b [1960].

Lafont, Bernard. *Au ciel de Verdun. Notes d'un aviateur.* Paris: Berger-Levrazt, 1918.

Lanham, Richard A. *A Handlist of Rhetorical Terms.* Berkeley: University of California Press, 1991.

Laplanche, Jean, and Jean-Bertrand Pontalis. *The Language of Psychoanalysis*, translated by Donald Nicholson Smith. London: Karnac Books, 1988 [1967].

Laplanche, Jean, and Jean-Bertrand Pontalis. *Vocabulaire de la psychanalyse.* Paris: Presses Universitaires de France, 2009 [1967].

Lauzon, Claudette. *The Unmaking of Home in Contemporary Art.* Toronto: Toronto Univesity Press, 2017.

Le Poulichet, Sylvie. *Psychanalyse de l'informe: Dépersonnalisations, addictions, traumatismes.* Paris: Flammarion, 2009.

Leroux, Gaston. *Le Fantôme de l'Opéra.* Paris: Presses de la Cité, 2008 [1910].

Leroux, Gaston. *The Phantom of the Opera*, translated by David Coward. Oxford: Oxford University Press, 2012 [1910].

Lewe, Christiane, Tim Othold, and Nicolas Oxen, eds. *Müll. Interdisziplinäre Perspektiven auf das Übrig-Gebliebene.* Bielefeld: transcript Verlag, 2016.

Liboiron, Max. "Why 'Discard Studies'? Why not 'Waste Studies'?" *Discard Studies.* April 9, 2014. Available online: https://discardstudies.com/201 4/09/04/why-discard-studies-why-not-waste-studies-2/ (accessed March 23, 2019).

Lindner, Christoph, and Miriam Meissner, eds. *Global Garbage: Urban Imaginaries of Waste, Excess, and Abandonment.* London and New York: Routledge, 2016.

Luko, Alexis. *Sonatas, Screams, and Silence: Music and Sound in the Films of Ingmar Bergman.* New York: Routledge, 2016.

Lyotard, Jean-François. *Discourse, Figure*, translated by Mary Lydon and Antony Hudek. Minneapolis: University of Minnesota Press, 2011 [1971].

Maclean, Mairi. *Michel Tournier: Exploring Human Relationships.* Bristol: Bristol Academic Press, 2003.

Magid, Václav. "A May Morning and the Struggle with an Enemy, against Which Victory Is Defeat." In *Jan Šerých Was Born on 24. 6. 2083 Minus One*, edited by Karel Císař, 99–113. Prague: Tranzit, 2008.

Malabou, Catherine. *The Future of Hegel: Plasticity, Temporality and Dialectic*, translated by Lisabeth During. London and New York: Routledge, 2005 [1996].

Malabou, Catherine. *Plasticity at the Dusk of Writing: Dialectic, Destruction, Deconstruction*, translated by Carolyn Shread. New York: Columbia University Press, 2010 [2005].

Málek, Petr. *Melancholie moderny.* Praha: Dauphin, 2008.

Masschelein, Anneleen. *The Unconcept: The Freudian Uncanny in Late-Twentieth-Century Theory.* New York: Suny Press, 2011.

Massumi, Brian. *Parables for the Virtual: Movement, Affect, Sensation*. Durham and London: Duke University Press, 2002.
Maurer, Naomi Margolis. *The Pursuit of Spiritual Wisdom: The Thought and Art of Vincent van Gogh and Paul Gauguin*. London: Fairleigh Dickinson University Press, 1998.
Mazanec, Martin. "Interview with Michal Pěchouček." *Labyrint revue* 11, no. 21–22 (2007): 86–8.
Menninghaus, Winfried. *In Praise of Nonsense: Kant and Bluebeard*, translated by Henry Pickford. Stanford: Stanford University Press, 1999.
Mersch, Dieter. "Meta/Dia: Two Different Approaches to the Medial." *Cultural Studies* 30, no. 4 (2016 [2010]): 650–679.
Mersch, Dieter. "Tertium Datur," *MATRIZes* 7, no. 1 (2013): 207–2.
Metzger, Rainer, and Ingo F. Walther. *Vincent van Gogh: The Complete Paintings*. Cologne and New York, 1997.
Michel, Marianne Roland. *Lajoüe et l'art rocaille*. Neuilly-sur-Seine: Arthena, 1984.
Miller, John Hillis: "Figure." In *Perspectives croisées sur la figure. À la rencontre du lisible et du visible*, edited by Bertrand Gervais and Audrey Lemieux, 53–7. Montréal: Presses de l'Université du Québec, 2012.
Mitchell, W. J. T. *Picture Theory: Essays on Verbal and Visual Representation*. Chicago: University of Chicago Press, 1994.
Morris, Paul D. *Vladimir Nabokov: Poetry and the Lyric Voice*. Toronto: University of Toronto Press, 2011.
Morrison, Susan Signe. *The Literature of Waste: Material Ecopoetics and Ethical Matter*. New York: Palgrave Macmillan, 2015.
Moser, Walter. "The Acculturation of Waste," translated by Brian Neville. In *Waste-Site Stories: The Recycling of Memory*, edited by Brian Neville and Johanne Villeneuve, 85–103. Albany: State University of New York Press, 2002.
Nabokov, Vladimir. *Pnin*. New York: Vintage International, 1989 [1957].
Nancy, Jean-Luc. *Le Regard du portrait*. Paris: Galilée, 2000.
Nancy, Jean-Luc. *L'Autre Portrait*. Paris: Galilée, 2014.
Nancy, Jean-Luc. *The Portrait*, translated by Sarah Clift and Simon Sparks. New York: Fordham University Press, 2018.
Navratil, Leo. *Schizophrénie et art*. Bruxelles: Presses Universitaires de France, 1978.
Nichols, David P., ed. *Van Gogh among the Philosophers: Painting, Thinking, Being*. Lanham: Lexington Books, 2017.
Nyberg, Dorothea: *Oeuvre de Juste Aurèle Meissonnier*. New York: Benjamin Blom Publishers, 1969.
Owens, Craig. "Representation, Appropriation, and Power." In *Beyond Recognition: Representation, Power and Culture*, edited by Scott Bryson, Barbara Kruger, Lynne Tillman, and Jane Weinstock, 88–113. Berkeley: University of California Press, 1992 [1982].
Parikka, Jussi. *A Geology of Media*. Minneapolis: University of Minnesota Press, 2015.

Pearl, Sharrona. *Face/On: Face Transplants and the Ethics of the Other.* Chicago: University of Chicago Press, 2017.

Petit, Susan. *Michel Tournier's Metaphysical Fictions.* Amsterdam: John Benjamins, 1991.

Pickvance, Ronald. *Van Gogh in Arles.* New York: Metropolitan Museum of Art, 1984.

Plana, Muriel. "Des monstres, des spectres, des écrans: Forme du mythe et mythe de la forme dans P.O.M.P.E.I., 2ème fouille de Caterina Sagna." In *De l'informe, du Difforme, du Conforme au théâtre. Sur la scène européenne, en Italie et en France,* edited by Yannick Butel, 15–33. Caen: Peter Lang; Université de Caen, 2010.

Plato. *Republic,* translated by C. D. C. Reeve. Indianapolis: Hackett Publishing Company, 2004.

Platten, David. *Michel Tournier and the Metaphor of Fiction.* Liverpool: Liverpool University Press, 1999.

Porter, James I. "Disfigurations: Erich Auerbach's Theory of Figura." *Critical Inquiry* 44, no. 1 (2017): 80–113.

Portmann, Adolf. *Animal Forms and Patterns: A Study of the Appearance of Animals,* translated by Hella Czech. London: Faber & Faber, 1964 [1948].

Pospiszyl, Tomaš. "The Treachery of Words," In *Jan Šerých Was Born on 24. 6. 2083 Minus One,* edited by Karel Císař, 45–51. Prague: Tranzit, 2008.

Proust, Marcel. *Swann's Way;* edited by Christopher Prendergast; translated by Lydia Davis. London: Penguin Classic, 2003

Rabaté, Jean-Michel. *The Cambridge Introduction to Literature and Psychoanalysis.* New York: Cambridge University Press, 2014.

Rabaté, Jean-Michel. *Rust.* London and New York: Bloomsbury, 2018.

Rathje, William, and Cullen Murphy. *Rubbish! The Archeology of Garbage.* Tucson: The University of Arizona Press, 2001.

Rémi, Henriette. *Hommes sans visage.* Lausanne: SPES, 1942.

Richter, Gerhard. *Walter Benjamin and the Corpus of Autobiography.* Detroit: Wayne State University, 2012.

Rilke, Rainer Maria. *The Notebooks of Malte Laurids Brigge,* translated by Stephen Mitchell. New York: Vintage Books, 1990 [1910].

Rilke, Rainer Maria. *Die Aufzeichnungen des Malte Laurids Brigge.* Berlin: Insel Verlag, 2012 [1910].

Rodowick, David N. *Reading for the Figural, or, Philosophy after the New Media.* Durham and London: Duke University Press, 2001.

Rogers, Annie G. "In the 'I' of Madness: Shifting Subjectivities in Girls and Women Psychological Development in the Yellow Wallpaper." In *Analyzing the Different Voice: Feminist Psychological Theory and Literary Texts,* edited by Jerilyn Fisher and Ellen S. Silber, 45–66. Lanham: Rowman & Littlefield Publishers, 1998.

Scanlan, John. *On Garbage.* London: Reaktion Books, 2005.

Scarry, Alaine. *The Body in Pain: The Making and Unmaking of the World.* New York: Oxford University Press, 1987.

Schmitt, Jean-Claude. "For a History of the Face: Physiognomy, Pathognomy, Theory of Expression." *Zeitschrift für Kunst- und Kulturwissenchaft* 40, no. 1 (2012): 7–20.

Scruton, Roger. *The Aesthetics of Music.* Oxford: Oxford University Press, 1997.

Shanks, Michael, David Platt, and William L. Rathje. "The Perfume of Garbage: Modernity and the Archaeological." *Modernism/Modernity* 11, no. 1 (2004): 61–83.

Shaviro, Steven. *Post-Cinematic Affect.* New York: Zero Books, 2010.

Siegert, Bernhard: *Cultural Techniques: Grids, Filters, Doors, and Other Articulations of the Real,* translated by Geoffrey Winthrop-Young. New York: Fordham University Press, 2015.

Silguy, Catherine de. *Histoire des hommes et de leurs ordures: du Moyen Âge à nos jours.* Paris: Le Cherche Midi, 2009.

Skinner, Quentin. "Paradiastole: Redescribing the Vices as Virtues." In *Renaissance Figures of Speech,* edited by Sylvia Adamson, Gavin Alexander, and Katrin Ettenhuber, 149–66, Cambridge: Cambridge University Press, 2007.

Slaby, Jan. "Relational Affect: Perspectives from Philosophy and Cultural Studies." In *How to Do Things with Affects: Affective Triggers in Aesthetic Forms and Cultural Practices,* edited by Ernst van Alphen and Tomáš Jirsa, 59–81. Leiden: Brill, 2019a.

Slaby, Jan. "Affective Arrangement." In *Affective Societies: Key Concepts,* edited by Jan Slaby and Christian von Scheve, 109–18. New York: Routledge, 2019b.

Slaby, Jan, and Rainer Mühlhoff. "Affect." In *Affective Societies: Key Concepts,* edited by Jan Slaby and Christian von Scheve, 27–41. New York: Routledge, 2019.

Smith, Douglas. "Disfigurements: Bacon, Deleuze, Lynch and the Formless." In *Formless: Ways In and Out of Form,* edited by Patrick Crowley and Paul Hegarty, 215–28. Bern: Peter Lang, 2005.

Sontag, Susan. *Regarding the Pain of Others.* New York: Farrar, Straus and Giroux, 2003.

Souriau, Étienne. *Vocabulaire d'esthétique.* Paris: Presses Universitaires de France, 2004 [1990].

Spinoza, Benedict de. *A Spinoza Reader: The Ethics and Other Works,* edited and translated by Edwin Curley. Princeton, NJ: Princeton University Press, 1994.

St. Jean, Shawn. "Hanging 'The Yellow Wall-Paper': Feminism and Textual Studies," *Feminist Studies* 28, no. 2 (2002): 396–415.

Starobinski, Jean. *The Invention of Liberty: 1700–1789,* Geneva: Skira, 1987 [1964].

Sylvester, David. *The Brutality of Fact: Interviews with Francis Bacon.* London: Thames and Hudson, 1993 [1975].

Sypher, Wylie. *Rococo to Cubism in Art and Literature*. New York: Random House, 1960.

The Oxford English Dictionary. Online edition. Oxford: Oxford University Press (Accessed on: February 8, 2019).

Thibaut-Pomerantz, Carolle. *Wallpaper: A History of Style and Trends*, translated by Deke Dusinberre and Carolle Thibaut-Pomerantz. Paris: Flammarion, 2009.

Thom, René. "Pouvoirs de la forme." In *Les Figures de la forme*, edited by Jean Gayon and Jean-Jacques Wunenburger, 17–26. Paris: L'Harmattan, 1992.

Thom, René. *Structural Stability and Morphogenesis: An Outline of a General Theory of Models*, translated by D. H. Fowler. Boca Raton: Taylor & Francis, 2018 [1972].

Thomas, Alfred. 1995. *The Labyrinth of the Word: Truth and Representation in Czech Literature*. München: Oldenbourg.

Tomkins, Silvan. "The Phantasy Behind the Face." *Exploring Affect: The Selected Writings of Silvan S. Tomkins*, edited by Virginia E. Demos, 263–78. Cambridge: Cambridge University Press, 1995 [1975].

Tournier, Michel. *The Wind Spirit: An Autobiography*, translated by A. Goldhammer. Boston: Beacon Press, 1988.

Tournier, Michel. *Gemini*, translated by Ann Carter. Baltimore and London: John Hopkins University, 1998 [1975].

Tournier, Michel. *Les Météores*. Paris: Gallimard, 2011 [1975].

Trakl, Georg. *A Skeleton Plays Violin*. Translated by James Reidel. New York: Seagull Books, 2017.

Vicks, Meghan. *Narratives of Nothing in 20th-Century Literature*. New York and London: Bloomsbury, 2015.

Viney, William. *Waste: A Philosophy of Things*. New York: Bloomsbury, 2014.

Voss, Christiane. "Affect Is the Medium." In *How to Do Things with Affects: Affective Triggers in Aesthetic Forms and Cultural Practices*, edited by Ernst van Alphen and Tomáš Jirsa, 200–15. Leiden: Brill, 2019.

Weidlé, Wladimir. "Biology of Art: Initial Formulation and Primary Orientation," translated by Elaine P. Halperin. *Diogenes* 7, no. 17 (1957 [1957]): 1–15.

Weinar, Adam. *By Authors Possessed: The Demoniac Novel in Russia*. Evanston: Northwestern University Press, 1998.

Weiner, Richard. "Prázdná židle." In *Spisy 1: Netečný divák a jiné prózy. Lítice. Škleb*, edited by Zina Trochová, 370–91. Prague: Torst, 1996a [1916].

Weiner, Richard. "Smazaný obličej." In *Spisy 1: Netečný divák a jiné prózy. Lítice. Škleb*, edited by Zina Trochová, 317–41. Prague: Torst, 1996b [1919].

Weiner, Richard. *The Game for Real*, translated by Benjamin Paloff. San Francisco: Two Lines Press, 2015 [1933].

Weisgerber, Jean. *Les masques fragiles. Esthétiques et formes de la littérature rococo*. Lausanne: L'Age d'homme, 1991.

Weiss, Judith Elisabeth. "Before and After the Portrait: Faces between Hidden Likeness and Anti-Portrait." In *Inventing Faces: Rhetorics of Portraiture between Renaissance and Modernism*, edited by Mona Körte, Ruben Rebmann, Judith Elisabeth Weiss, and Stefan Weppelmann, 133–46. Berlin: Deutscher Kunstverlag, 2013.

Widera, Steffi. *Richard Weiner. Identität und Polarität im Prosafrühwerk.* München: Verlag Otto Sagner, 2001.

Withy, Katherine. *Heidegger on Being Uncanny.* Cambridge, MA, and London: Harvard University Press, 2015.

Wittgenstein, Ludwig. *Philosophical Investigations*, edited by P. M. S. Hacker and Joachim Schulte; translated by G. E. M. Anscombe, P. M. S. Hacker, and Joachim Schulte. Oxford: Blackwell, 2009 [1953].

Wolfe, Cary. "Language." In *Critical Terms for Media Studies*, edited by W. J. T. Mitchell and Mark Hansen, 233–48. Chicago: The University of Chicago Press, 2010.

Worton, Michael. *La Goutte d'or.* University of Glasgow French and German Publications: Castle Carry Press, 1992.

Worton, Michael, ed. *Michel Tournier.* New York: Routledge, 2014.

Žižek, Slavoj. "Grimaces of the Real, or When the Phallus Appears." *October*, no. 58 (Autumn, 1991): 44–68.

Žižek, Slavoj. *The Ticklish Subject*: The Absent Centre of Political Ontology. New York: Verso, 2000 [1997].

Žižek, Slavoj. *Enjoy Your Symptom! Jacques Lacan in Hollywood and Out.* London and New York: Routledge, 2008a.

Žižek, Slavoj. "Psychoanalysis and the Lacanian Real: 'Strange shapes of the unwarped primal world.'" In *Adventures in Realism*, edited by Matthew Beaumont, 207–23. Oxford: Blackwell Publishing, 2008b.

Žižek, Slavoj. *Living in the End Times.* London: Verso, 2010.

Zusi, Peter. "States of Shock: Kafka and Richard Weiner." In *Kafka, Prag und der Erste Weltkrieg / Kafka, Prague and the First World War* (Oxford Kafka Studies 2), edited by Manfred Engel and Ritchie Robertson, 127–42. Würzburg: Königshausen & Neumann, 2012.

INDEX

abject   29, 121 n.5, 121 n.7
absence
  bodily   21, 92, 104
  double   94–5 (*see also*
    Zusi, Peter)
  of form   34
  formal work of   97–8
  mediality of   105, 107 (*see
    also* Chairs)
  between presence and   28, 33,
    96, 108
  presence made of   93, 98, 107
    (*see also* Lacan, Jacques)
  the present   18, 105, 107, 112,
    128 n.12
  of the subject   91–6, 98, 102–5,
    107–11 (*see also* portrait
    of absence)
  the trace of   101, 104
Adorno, Theodor W.   2, 15, 119 n.1
aesthetics
  camp   65
  ethics and   126 n.11
  of the formless   19, 25, 42, 114
  of the garbage   80–1
  of nothing   128 n.11
  rococo   55
  traditional   50, 69
affect
  between *affectus* and
    affectio   13, 15, 113
  affordances of forms and   20,
    54, 72
  beyond signification   11–13
  definitions of   4, 11–12, 120 n.9
  Deleuzian concept of   11, 13
  as distinct from emotions and
    feelings   10–11
  face as a site of   26–7, 40

formal work of   4, 14–16,
    19, 24, 28–30, 35, 68,
    113–14, 117
  intentional   29–30, 122 n.10
  operational qualities of   21,
    41, 113
  performative force of   2, 10, 15,
    24, 43, 62–3, 97–8, 105,
    111, 116–17
  relational approach to   13–15,
    41, 120 n.11 (*see also*
    Slaby, Jan)
  in Spinoza's *Ethics*   13
  structuring discourse   24–5,
    28, 33, 61, 106, 108–9,
    128 n.12
  theory   11–14, 21, 119 n.8
  turn to   10–13, 120 n.8
affective agency   2, 4, 7, 11–12,
    14–15, 17, 19, 21, 24–5,
    28, 33, 48, 54, 58, 68,
    113–14, 116
affective compounds   21, 54,
    113, 116–17
affective formalism   11–12, 14,
    25, 41, 113; *see also*
    Brinkema, Eugenie
affectively driven generative
    deformations   15, 118;
    see also disformations
affective operations   2–4, 10,
    12, 15, 18, 21, 102, 107,
    114–15, 118, 129 n.1
  revaluating   18, 20, 73, 80, 116
  saturating   18–19, 43–4, 55, 115
  shattering   18–19, 24, 32, 34, 41,
    43, 115
  shifting   18, 20, 92, 97, 105,
    108–11, 116

146

Index

Index

www.ingramcontent.com/pod-product-compliance
Lightning Source LLC
Chambersburg PA
CBHW050519280326
41932CB00014B/2384